in the c   M000227884

in the company
of men

Neil LaBute

Faber and Faber
BOSTON · LONDON

This screenplay was published by special arrangement with Stephen
Pevner, Inc., a Literary Agency, 248 West 73rd St., Second Floor, New
York, NY 10023 (212) 496-0474, FAX (212) 496-0796. All rights reserved.

A CIP record for this book is available from the Library of Congress.
ISBN 0-571-19931-3

Cover photography by François Dischinger

Printed in the United States of America

For my mother, who showed me the path
For Lisa, who lit the way
For Stephen, who paid most of the tolls

Neil LaBute (WRITER/DIRECTOR) is a graduate of Brigham Young University, University of Kansas and New York University. While enrolled in the Graduate Dramatic Writing Program at NYU, he was the recipient of a literary fellowship to study at the Royal Court Theatre in London and attended the Sundance Institute's Playwrights Lab. His other works include "Filthy Talk for Troubled Times," "Lepers," "Bash," "A Gaggle of Saints," "Rounder," "Sanguinarians & Sycophants," "Ravages," and adaptations of "Dracula" and "Woyzeck" which have been produced in the US and abroad. He lives in Fort Wayne, Indiana with his wife and two children.

INTERVIEW WITH
NEIL LABUTE

in the company of men **has been praised for its novel treatment of the classic love triangle. What were the origins of the screenplay?**
"Let's hurt somebody." That line of dialogue was the first idea in my mind. I was attracted to the notion of premeditated agony inflicted on someone. I believe that you can kill characters only once, but you can hurt them every day . . . My model for the screenplay was restoration comedy. The script has a five-act structure and is centered around wealthy, blasé characters who do unspeakable things just because they feel like it. It's a simple story: boys meet girl, boys crush girl, boys giggle.

It's difficult to classify *in the company of men* **into a set genre. Do you feel comfortable referring to the film as a black comedy?**
The film does have a lot of laughs. Then the situation turns vicious . . . I love the idea of pulling people in and then turning on them. For instance, seducing them into thinking that the character of Chad is amusing and even charming, only to leave them shocked when they discover later just how much of a viper he really is.

Chad is a misogynist and a racist. He betrays and hurts both Christine and Howard. Why isn't Chad punished for his actions in the end?
It always seemed more potent to let Chad get away with everything. That gives the film a punch at the end that some people are taken aback by: the expectation is to make him or her feel that the world is not right. We live in a "cause and effect" world. We tend to carry this idea over into movies. For many viewers, it's just not fair that Chad gets away.

Do you think female viewers might be so angered by the misogynistic attitudes of the male characters that it would negatively affect their feelings toward the film itself?

No, not really. One woman even told me she thought *in the company of men* was the most feminist movie that she had ever seen.

Although Howard becomes a victim of Chad's plan to "restore dignity" into the two men's frustrated lives, isn't his character just as despicable?

I personally have more disgust for Howard. He gets into a situation that he could have avoided. There are moments where he could redeem himself and he doesn't. He ends up saying far worse things to Christine than Chad ever does.

What was the purpose of making Christine deaf?

Words are weapons for both Chad and Howard. For that reason, it was more interesting for Christine to have a difficulty with the power of speech. By being deaf, she's not just being preyed upon as a woman . . . She's a sympathetic character, but she never asks for any kind of pity. That seems to put people off guard. They think just because she's deaf that she's going to be more fragile. In fact, she is fairly outgoing and strong.

Do you think that the character of Chad reassures men by making them feel they're not as bad as him?

Possibly. But not everyone is completely turned off by Chad. His character is not without charm. Some might even admire him for the audacity of what he does. So much of that has to be credited to the performance and steely assurance of Aaron Eckhart, the actor who plays Chad.

Do you think that the retro-sexism seen in the film is becoming increasingly more present in today's society?

I don't think that sexism necessarily ever went away at all. Of course, during the past twenty years we've started to overcome those archaic notions about a "woman's place." But at the same time, I think it is ludicrous to insist that people who are better-educated are likely to be less sexist or racist. Old tricks die hard. An education often refines hatred. A lot of people in the eighties and nineties have picked up a couple of diplomas, but it hasn't changed their overall moral structure.

Did you have particular reasons for choosing the business world as the environment for *in the company of men*?
That sort of nameless, faceless corporate environment seemed to me the ideal setting for Chad and Howard to pull off their scam. Modern offices can be so compartmentalized with those horrible, carpeted half-barriers which seem to turn workers into numbers.

Were you trying to paint a portrait of an amoral, uncaring contemporary society?
Yes. In the corporate world, people tend to adopt a siege mentality. Today's business philosophies are comprised of just a few catch phrases—'take control,' 'watch your back,' 'go for it' . . . After a sixteen-hour work day, it's hard to shift gears and become a person again, to realize things like 'love is not a commodity' and 'it's okay to lose.'

Has the scene in which Chad forces a young African-American intern to literally show that he "has the balls" for the job received controversial reactions?
Yes, some viewers have been taken aback by how Chad's desire for humiliation and control actually force the intern into doing what he does. I think most are surprised by the degree to where the scene goes. It keeps notching itself up further and further. It starts with the general degrading of someone on a cultural level then on to a sexually-specific humiliation. I wanted to show the breadth of Chad's anger, hatred, and need to control in every scene and with every kind of person. Chad's venom is not limited to any one kind of person.

What messages were you trying to send out about the film's issues, for example, misogyny and racism?
I never set out to make this film a statement about any one particular theme and hopefully everyone will carry away something different. A film like this would have done itself a disservice to tie things up in a simple package . . . The film is certainly meant to broach more questions than answers and I feel no obligation to

answer any of those questions. My attitude is that since I went to the trouble of raising the questions, it's up to the viewer to decide on the answers on his or her own.

Isn't that a dangerous stand to take as a filmmaker?
It can be. If a writer-director decides not to reveal and simply to present, he runs the risk of being questioned on his personal ethics and moral base.

It's difficult to place the film in any particular year. How do you explain this?
I'm intrigued by minimalism and I wanted the look of the film to have an antiseptic and timeless feel. The business world has looked relatively the same since the fifties, turning it into a bit of a cliché, so I tried stylistically to be very timeless. The men wear nondescript white shirts and ties. I didn't use a lot of outdoor shots. I shot about seventy-five percent of the interiors in the Lincoln Tower, an art deco building which was a model for the Empire State Building. It helped add to the film's timeless feel.

What was your primary concern during the shoot?
I just wanted to tell the story. For my first feature, I had no intention of trying to include everything I ever thought of doing on film. There are no complicated camera moves in the film. I prefer visuals driven by the story. I like actors and I like long takes. I like the idea of just sitting back and watching, almost voyeuristically, what's going on between the characters. Ultimately, your primary concern during a shoot becomes staying out of the way and letting the magic happen.

CAST

CHAD	Aaron Eckhart
CHRISTINE	Stacy Edwards
HOWARD	Matt Malloy
CO-WORKER 1	Michael Martin
JOHN	Mark Rector
CO-WORKER 2	Chris Hayes
INTERN	Jason Dixie
SUZANNE	Emily Cline

CAST

WRITER/DIRECTOR	Neil LaBute
PRODUCERS	Mark Archer
	Stephen Pevner
DIRECTOR OF PHOTOGRAPHY	Tony Hettinger
EDITOR	Joel Plotch
MUSIC	Ken Williams
	Karel Roessingh
SOUND DESIGN	Tony Moskal
	George Moskal
EXECUTIVE PRODUCERS	Toby Gaff
	Mark Hart
	Matt Malloy
LINE PRODUCER	Lisa Bartels
ASSOCIATE PRODUCER	Joyce Pierpoline
PRODUCTION DESIGNER	Julia Henkel
1ST ASSISTANT DIRECTOR	Denise Snider
2ND AD	Patrick Veverka
1ST AC	John "J.T." Thorn
2ND AC	Paul Wilson, Jr.
KEY GRIP	Manuel Dominguez
GAFFER	Laurent "Thor" Weber
GRIPS	Ngozi Rejane Rogers
	Amber Herrmann
	John Hartman
	Tiffany Kostov

1

SOUND RECORDIST	Guy Camara
SOUND ASSISTANT	Adam Marshall
LOCATION CASTING	Atlantis Entertainment
MAKE UP	Joe Moyer
GRIP/PA	Cheryl Russel
KEY/PA	Jason Dixie
PA	Joe Koenig
RUNNER	Cheryl Russell
CATERING	Sara Kiser
STILL PHOTOS	Jason Savage
PRODUCTION OFFICE	The Office Alternative
FILM PROCESSING	CineFilm Laboratories
VIDEO DAILIES	CineTransfer
COLOR TIMING	Kenny Becker
NEGATIVE DATABASE	Michael Phillips
NEGATIVE CUTTING	Northeast Negative Matchers, Inc.
VIDEO CONFORM	Stephen Mahan
VIDEO FACILITY	On Track Video, NYC
AUDIO POST PRODUCTION	Legacy Sound Ltd., Victoria B.C.
MIXING ENGINEER	Tony Moskal
FOLEY ARTISTS	Susan Kelsey
	Lana Hunter
	George Moskal
FOLEY EDITOR	Tony Moskal
ASSISTANT ENGINEER	Kirby Walker
TITLES	F-Stop Studio/NYC
MUSIC RECORDED AT	Legacy Studios, Victoria B.C.
MUSIC PRODUCER/MIXER	Tony Moskal
PRODUCTION COUNSEL	Donna L. Bascom, Esq.
CREATIVE CONSULTANT	Lisa Gore
BEST GIRL	Kristina Gore Trevail

in the company of men made its world premiere at the Sundance Film Festival, where it won the Filmmakers Trophy for Best Dramatic Feature in Competition.

SILENCE. DARKNESS.

THE ROAR OF TRIBAL MUSIC OVER CREDITS.

INT. TOWN AIRPORT SMOKING LOUNGE—MORNING

Upscale oasis for travelers, tourists and teetotalers. All soft neon and reflective surfaces. A BUSINESS CROWD *mingles easily with itself as* A COMMUTER AIRPLANE *lifts off just outside one tinted window, shaking the glass and providing a momentary spectacle for anyone sober enough to care. Few do.*

CHAD *sits at a nearby bench seat, comfortably toying with his Zippo; 29 years old, dark, tallish. The mouth of Belmondo and the eyes of Caligula. He watches the others, caught up in the their energy, but he is not one of them. From time to time he steals a glance in both directions and at his watch, slowly caressing the tip of a cigarette between his lips.*

A moment later HOWARD *joins him, holding a moistened napkin to one ear and carefully swabbing at the tender flesh while keeping a suspicious eye turned to the hallway. He is 28, more boyishly attractive than handsome, perhaps shorter than he might wish to be.* CHAD *glances over at him upon his return, smiling and speaking softly.*

> CHAD
>
> . . . So. How's it feel?

> HOWARD
>
> 'S okay.

> CHAD
>
> Yeah?

> HOWARD
>
> 'S alright. Hurts a little . . .

> CHAD
>
> Where'd she get you?

> HOWARD
>
> Right here . . .

> CHAD
>
> 'S no blood. Not a mark, anything . . .

3

HOWARD

Still feel it.

CHAD

Sure. (*beat*) See, this is the point I was making earlier . . .

HOWARD

What?

CHAD

The '90s. Can't even afford to blink . . . I miss too much.

HOWARD

No big deal . . .

CHAD

Howard, a woman hit you! Tagged you upside the head, and for what? What'd you say to her?

HOWARD

Nothing.

CHAD

You said nothing?

HOWARD

Asked her the time. 'S all . . .

CHAD

"The time." (*beat*) "What time is it?" or "You got the time?" 'S a crucial difference . . .

HOWARD

I asked her what time it was. She had a watch on . . .

CHAD *nods at this, casually pointing to* HOWARD*'s Rolex and laughing.*

HOWARD

. . . I'm not kidding.

CHAD

Wait, wait, wait a minute . . . you're telling me about some sorta unprovoked assault here? That is uncalled for! (*beat*) She give you the time at least?

4

HOWARD

No.

TWO WOMEN LAUGHING *can be heard as they move off.* CHAD *watches them go, disgusted.*

CHAD

What the fuck are you laughing at?!

HOWARD

Just let it go, Chad . . . it's not worth it.

CHAD

Okay, well, we're doomed then . . . you know? Seriously. As a race, men like us, guys who care a smidgeon about the work-place, their women. We are doomed if this is how they're gonna treat us . . .

HOWARD

Who do you mean?

CHAD

Everybody! I mean, look at us—sitting in some courtesy lounge, middle of the week and time just passing us by—completely at the whim of those bastards upstairs . . . (*touches* HOWARD*'s ear*) . . . and now this.

HOWARD

Oww! (*feels it himself*) . . . yeah.

CHAD

Life is for the taking, is it not? I mean, we're, like, ten years out 'a university, that's all, just ten . . . and I got a whole crop 'a these young dudes after my desk. Taking jobs as production assistants—title didn't even exist two years ago!—just to hang out in the coffee room, bunch 'a vultures waiting for me to tire out. Low numbers two months in a row? Huh? They're gonna feed on my insides . . . I'm no fool, okay?

HOWARD

'Course not.

CUT TO:

INT. TOWN AIRPORT WAITING AREA—A BIT LATER

Endless rows of maroon bench seats. Flights zooming past the picture windows. A few PATRONS *waiting for planes, saying goodbye, or sleeping upright.*

CHAD *sits with his legs up, eating a cookie.* HOWARD *hunched near him, supporting a laptop on his knees.* CHAD *yawns.*

> CHAD
>
> New guy's okay, though, huh?

> HOWARD
>
> Looks like it.

> CHAD
>
> Sure he is . . .

> HOWARD
>
> Kind 'a funny, actually . . .

> CHAD
>
> Don't doubt it.

> HOWARD
>
> Big guy. Played ball, I hear . . .

> CHAD
>
> Uh-huh, and probably bought everybody lunch on Wednesday . . .

> HOWARD
>
> Yeah, he did.

> CHAD
>
> And that's all well and wonderful and funny stories about his girlfriend in the sack, I bet he spins a good one. But you watch . . . a year from now he'll be asking you to toss around ideas with some 'a the junior staff, and "Would you mind leaving me the cruller? 'S the only donut I like." Telling you now, Howard, be careful . . .

6

HOWARD

Okay. (*stops typing a moment*) Yeah, I . . . okay.

CHAD

What're you working on there . . . (*reads over his friend's shoulder*) . . . checking how "Project Director" looks on your letterhead?

HOWARD

Nah. (*laughs*) Just going over these . . .

CHAD

Forget it, I'm kidding you. (*beat*) Anyway, just watch this guy's ass, that's all I'm saying.

HOWARD

Sure.

CHAD

'Cause he's new and clever and hell of a shortstop, Fourth of July picnic . . . 'til the company has a slight recession and he's bandying your name around as somebody for "the Phoenix office." And he's off collecting another woodgrain plaque, "Employee of the Month . . ."

HOWARD

Right. I'll be careful . . .

CHAD

'S all I'm telling you. Watch your back . . .

CUT TO:

INT. TOWN AIRPORT HALLWAY—THAT EVENING

Long strip of motorized walkway. Medium-sized Midwestern airport. A few TRAVELERS *ride the rails or walk along, personal belongings under their arms.*

CHAD *and* HOWARD, *standing still and moving slowly with the flow. Each with a suitcase and a hanging clothes bag.* CHAD *yawns once again.*

7

HOWARD

Seeing a girl for almost a year . . . well, you met her. Maybe six months ago, that seafood place?

CHAD

Little brunette? Melody something . . .

HOWARD

Uh-huh. Well, Melanie . . .

CHAD

Cute. Very cute, as I remember . . .

HOWARD

Yep. (*beat*) Even gave her a ring, weekend up at the Cape . . . introduced her to the folks.

CHAD

Serious?

HOWARD

Oh yeah. I really liked her . . .

CHAD

Sounds it.

HOWARD

But then she starts the "gotta see other people" setup and that whole routine . . . and I'm parking outside her house at four in the morning, going in to work circles under my eyes, call her three times before she calls me back once, you know, the whole "phone fade-out" thing . . . and finally I say, "This is not needed in my life. I don't need this." (*beat*) Somebody rejects me, you know, a woman, it just drives me, ahh! It just seems like everything, I mean . . . work, these women . . . feels like things are getting out 'a balance, don't they?

CHAD

Yeah, they do, Howard, they really do . . .

CUT TO:

INT. COMMUTER AIRPLANE—LATER STILL

8

A narrow hallway of formed plastic and multicolored cloth seats. Claustrophobic as hell, even with only a few other PASSENGERS *on board.*
A FEMALE FLIGHT ATTENDANT *moves purposefully along.*

CHAD *and* HOWARD *sit in opposing aisle seats, watching and waiting.*
HOWARD *tries to scan a document but can't keep focused on it.*

> CHAD

But you know what? Know why I'm still chipper, big grin on my face, Howie?

> HOWARD

Why's that?

> CHAD

'Cause I realized something. Figured this thing out about a month ago. (*beat*) Came home and Suzanne had packed up the joint. Yeah . . . just gone.

> HOWARD

Really? You never . . .

> CHAD

Uh-huh. Left me a futon and my poster of *American Gigolo*— bitch even took the frame off of it!—and I'm standing there, no note, not a "Thanks for four years of a roof over my bleached-blonde head," not anything. And it comes to me . . . the truth. (*beat*) I do not give a shit. Not about anybody. A family member. The job. None of it. Couldn't care less . . .

HOWARD *studies his friend at this, sorry to hear the news. The lights overhead flicker a moment as bursts of white and dark flicker across their faces.* HOWARD *looks up but* CHAD *faces straight ahead.*

> HOWARD

Geez . . .

> CHAD

Get me wrong . . . we're pals. Always have been.

> HOWARD

Same college . . .

9

CHAD

Exactly. And that means something . . . but these other folks, jump on while the going's good, no. Uh-uh. That will not do . . . (*beat*) People. Goddamn Suzanne, probably in Arizona right now, riding dune buggies, not a care on this earth. God, that really just makes me wanna fuck somebody up, but good! . . .

HOWARD

Geez . . .

CUT TO:

INT. TOWN AIRPORT COURTESY VAN—LATER THAT EVENING

Brightly colored van zipping along a two-lane. No one inside except the DRIVER, CHAD, *and* HOWARD. *The two younger men sit in the back, huddled together and staring out their respective windows. Woods and farmland alternate across the horizon.* CHAD *studies this, shaking his head, while* HOWARD *appears lost in thought.*

CHAD

You know, if we were living in India . . . you could've burned that fiancee of yours on a pyre in the village square, even hinting at what she did to you. To this day . . .

HOWARD

I hear you.

CHAD

Circle the date on this one, big guy . . . we keep on playing along with this "pick up the check, can't a girl change her mind?" crap, and we can't even tell a joke in the workplace?! . . . there is gonna be hell to pay down the line, no doubt about it. We need to put our foot down, pronto. (*beat*) Never lose control. 'S the key, Howard, that is the total key to the universe. Trust me . . .

CUT TO:

INT. TOWN HOTEL BAR—THE WEE HOURS

Moderately priced theme bar. '50s decor. CHAD *and* HOWARD, *still in their work duds, sit in a booth and nurse mixed drinks. A* COCKTAIL WAITRESS *moves past without stopping as* CHAD *holds up his glass. She doesn't even blink.*

> HOWARD

Ahh . . .

> CHAD

Come on . . .

> HOWARD

I dunno . . .

ANOTHER WAITRESS *appears with a pitcher, standing over them.* CHAD *studies her a moment before speaking.*

> CHAD

Do we look like frat boys to you? We need scotch . . .

She wanders off, looking for the correct table and a bit taken aback. CHAD *watches her go, then returns to* HOWARD.

> CHAD

Listen, we're in town for six weeks, right?—and I'm just talking now, so jump in—but what say . . . and this is perfect, what with the breakup thing you've got going, too . . . but say we were to find some gal—and I know we've got a shitload of stuff to get done, I know that, but for the sake of argument, let's just say we stumbled onto somebody, okay?—so, this person is just vulnerable as hell, right? Young thing, the wallflower type, whatever—or disfigured in some way, I don't know—but just some woman who is pretty sure that life . . . and I mean a full, healthy sexual life, romance, stuff like that . . . is lost to her forever. Okay?

Glasses slam down onto the table. The edge of an apron whisks past their faces as CHAD *grins and calls out after her.*

> CHAD

God bless you . . . (*to* HOWARD) Anyhow, we take a girl 'a that type—some cornfed bitch who'd practically mess her pants if you sharpen a pencil for her!—and we both hit her. Small talk.

11

A dinner date. And flowers. No pushing it, not all in her blouse first night out, but it's taking her out to see an ice show, something like that . . . and we just do it. You know? You and me, upping the ante, all the time . . . she's suddenly got two men! She's crazy with joy, she's wearing makeup again! And on we play, and on and on! (*beat*) And then one day, out goes the rug, and us pulling it hard and "Jill," she comes tumbling after . . .

The scotch stops dead halfway to HOWARD*'s mouth.* HOWARD, *taken aback, looks at* CHAD.

HOWARD

Whoooa . . .

CHAD

Hour later we are on a flight back to civilization like nothing happened. (*beat*) Trust me, she will be reaching for the sleeping pills within a week and we'll laugh about this 'til we're very old men . . . what do you think?

HOWARD

Well, it's . . .

CHAD

Is that not ideal? Restore a little dignity to our lives?! And the beauty is, for the next month and a half we can basically just rewrite the books. You know? I mean, play ourselves off as whoever the hell we wanna be, it's up to us . . .

HOWARD

Right, no, that sounds, ahh . . . yeah.

CHAD

I don't wanna shock you, Howard . . . 's just a thought. (*beat*) 'S really just the same crap we used to pull in school only it's better, 'cause we get a little payback on all this messy relationship shit we're dealing with . . . (*beat*) . . . think about it.

HOWARD

No, yeah . . . it's funny. It is. 'S just . . . way out there.

CHAD

Sure, and that's why it's so perfect . . . this is all virgin territory.
And no matter what happens after it—jumped over for promo-
tions, wife runs off with some biochemist, who knows what—
we'd always have this thing, just to fall back on. Could always
say, "Yeah, fine, but they never got me like we got her . . ." (*beat*)
I think it'd be refreshing, I really do. And very therapeutic,
coming off the women we just have . . .

HOWARD

Well, just for instance . . . who'd it be?

CHAD

No idea . . . but she's out there. I know it. Just waiting for us to
find her.

CUT TO:

INT. TOWN HOTEL HALLWAY—THE END OF THE NIGHT

Strip of well-lit carpet and doors. Gray and mauve dripping everywhere.
HOWARD *stands near a door as his friend opens it up.* CHAD *steps inside
and turns, a shadow falling across his face as he finishes telling a joke
to* HOWARD.

HOWARD

So what'd he say then?

CHAD

He says, "I don't trust anything that bleeds for a week and
doesn't die!" (*they burst out laughing*) . . . so. You in?

HOWARD

Oh, shit. Man. . . . (*thinking*) Yeah, I'm in.

CHAD

Then let's do it . . .

HOWARD *hesitates a moment longer, then smiles weakly and nods an
OK as he trudges off toward his next-door room and fumbles with a key
in the lock.* CHAD'*s lips curl up like he's slipping into Whoville as his own
door closes.*

CHAD
(*to himself*)

Let's hurt somebody.

CUT TO:

FADE IN:

TITLE: WEEK ONE

FADE OUT:

INT. COMPANY TYPING POOL—A MORNING OF THE FIRST WEEK

The roar of morning. Endless desks and computer keys being punched. The sound is deafening. Dozens of OFFICE WORKERS *mill about the place.* CHAD *moves across the floor, nodding or chatting with various* MEN. *Finally, he approaches* CHRISTINE, *who sits at a corner desk, earphones on and fingers flying. Attractive, mid-twenties, an air of sadness. She seems removed from the rest of the office frolic and frenzy, busily tapping away and reading from a stack of papers.* CHAD *comes up behind her, reading from a document, and begins talking as he nears her.*

CHAD
Hi, how are you? Listen . . . (*after a moment*) 'Scuse me?
(*to himself*) Jesus . . . what do I look like, the sandwich guy?
(*to Christine*) Excuse me?

A tap to CHRISTINE's *shoulder and she immediately turns, flashing an attractive smile and removing her earphones. In spite of himself,* CHAD *returns the smile and launches into his spiel.*

CHAD
Must be the headphones. Don't know how you work with music . . . that would drive me batty! (*beat*) Anyway, look, somebody pointed you out, said you were good, and I've got this . . . (*holds up document*) I need it by two. Gotta have it by two, and that's all there is. I'm not carrying this thing, in my hand, two o'clock . . . forget about it. I'll be sitting down here next to you tomorrow, asking to borrow your white-out. And I don't type . . . so. (*beat*) Think you can do it? Good . . .

14

A nod of yes from CHRISTINE *and she takes the manuscript. She smiles again and returns to the work at hand, forgoing her phones this time around.* CHAD *looks away and speaks again, but* CHRISTINE *only types without turning.*

> CHAD

Listen, just throw a cover sheet on it, grab one 'a those company folders and shove it in the . . . Excuse me?

A glance back reveals that she is not listening. Instead of pushing the issue, CHAD *mutters to himself and moves off.*

> CHAD

What the hell . . . did I roll in something?

CUT TO:

INT. COMPANY OFFICE—SAME TIME

A tangle of shelves, desks, and work areas. Expensive furnishings abound, but piled up with stacks of paper, reports, etc. A makeshift, windowless war room.

HOWARD *stands talking on the phone while* COWORKER 1 *thumbs through a magazine.*

> HOWARD

No. No, no. That's not it at all. No, it's not. No, that is not the point I'm making. No, it isn't! Don't tell me it is, I'm here, I'm talking to you right now and I'm telling you no, so it's not. No. No . . . look, we're not getting anywhere, because it's not, and I can't keep saying that because I'm not, and see, I'm working and this is a company line and we're going in circles here . . .
> *(he gestures for his coworker to exit)* No, I suggest you talk directly with her . . .

COWORKER 1 *smiles as* HOWARD *shakes his head, making a "crazy" sign with his finger and pointing at his head. Scooping up his reading material, the young man saunters out and leaves* HOWARD *to it.*

HOWARD

Mom . . . I said no. I don't care if she's been calling, doesn't mean I wanna call her back. No, it doesn't. It does not! Well, tell her to stop bothering you and give me a twenty-five cent call, she wants to chat so bad . . . (*beat*) No, I can't tell her! Then I'd have to call her, what do you think I don't want her new number for? So I don't have to be the one who . . . Mom, no! No . . . She said that? Really? I can't even . . . (*to himself*) That bitch. (*to mom*) No, I didn't. No, I didn't say that . . . I mean, I didn't mean it. I know . . . (*coworker enters*) I gotta go. We won't be needing your help. (*he hangs up*) Sales reps . . . aggressive little pricks.

CUT TO:

INT. COMPANY OFFICE—SAME TIME

A cardboard cutout of the last one, perhaps a bit tidier. A YOUNG MAN *sits at a desk, half-heartedly reading a series of graphs and munching on a hoagie.*

CHAD *appears at the doorway, glancing in and offering up a smile.*

CHAD

Hey, ahh, John, right?

JOHN

Uh-huh. How's it going?

CHAD

Fine . . .

JOHN

Good. (*beat*) How's the digs upstairs?

CHAD

Whaa . . . ? Oh, shitty. Don't even have a desk! Got these fucking painters wandering around . . .

JOHN

Yeah, well, least you got a window. (*beat*) They had a problem with the A/C a few weeks ago . . .

16

CHAD

Hmm. Well, let's just say it's a touch rustic . . . (*beat*) Anyway, listen, what is the story on that girl you sent me to? 'S acting like I got shit smeared on my tie . . .

JOHN *chuckles at this and grins up at* CHAD. CHAD *isn't amused.*

JOHN

Sorry, I shoulda said something. She's always like that . . .

CHAD

Yeah, well, it's annoying as hell! Can't hold a conversation two minutes . . . what kind 'a feminist twaddle is that? (*beat*) She think she is, some goddess?

JOHN

No . . . deaf.

CHAD *snaps to attention at this one, looking slyly back at his coworker.*

CHAD

You're shitting me. (*pointing up to his ears*) what about the headphones thing . . . ?

JOHN

I dunno . . . self-conscious, I guess. (*beat*) She pretty much keeps to herself, times I see her.

CHAD

No shit . . . thanks.

CHAD *mulls this over, then turns around and rockets back out the door.*

CUT TO:

INT. COMPANY TYPING POOL—SAME TIME

CHAD *stands at the back of the room, taking in the distance between himself and* CHRISTINE. *He clears his throat, then screams out.*

CHAD

HEY!!!!

17

Several typists and coworkers look up at the noise. They see CHAD *is watching* CHRISTINE, *who types on, oblivious to those around her. Most of them simply go back to work, although one* YOUNG MAN *near her makes "rabbit ears" behind* CHRISTINE's *head as he walks past.* CHAD *smiles at him and disappears;* CHRISTINE *just catches the guy behind her, but immediately returns to her work.*

CUT TO:

INT. COMPANY OFFICE—MOMENTS LATER

CHAD *reappears in the doorway, looking disbelievingly at his new pal. A grin meets him as he enters.*

> JOHN
>
> Do I lie?

> CHAD
>
> Jesus . . . what do you got 'a use to get her attention . . . like, a dog whistle?

> JOHN
>
> No! Reads lips . . .

> CHAD
>
> Great.

> JOHN
>
> Nice girl. (*beat*) She's been here, like, three weeks, placed by one of those agencies . . .

> CHAD
>
> Uh-huh.

> JOHN
>
> Types like ninety-five words a minute . . .

> CHAD
>
> Super. She speak at all?

> JOHN
>
> I've never heard her. I think she has one of those voices, you know, like . . .

18

CHAD

. . . yeah, like a dolphin.

A guffaw rises up from the two boys at this. CHAD *approximates a dolphin sound.*

CHAD

'S like having a Sunday chat with Flipper, that's what you're telling me . . . right? (*simulates sound*)

JOHN

Something like that.

CHAD

Oh, man . . . what a piece 'a work.

JOHN

She's kind of pretty, though. (*a moment passes*) . . . anyway.

CHAD

Yeah, anyway, thanks. (*dolphin voice*) See you later . . .

An explosion of laughter from them as CHAD *heads off.*

CUT TO:

INT. COMPANY TYPING POOL—THAT AFTERNOON

Back at CHRISTINE*'s desk.* CHAD *is just picking up his report and is practically beaming down at* CHRISTINE. *She smiles back, if a bit self-consciously.*

CHAD

This is great . . . (*reading*) Listen . . . about this morning. 'S very rude, I didn't even introduce myself. I'm Chad Piercewell. Nice to meet you . . . you're new here, aren't you?

CHRISTINE *looks at him and nods yes, grinning shyly.*

CHAD

Don't be embarrassed. We're all new some time, right? (*beat*) That's a lovely blouse . . .

19

CUT TO:

INT. COMPANY MEN'S ROOM—ANOTHER TIME

Gilded brass and expensive fixtures. Faux marble everywhere.

CHAD *stands at a full-length mirror, fly open and shirt untucked, studying himself.* HOWARD, *perched in a nearby stall, is smartly represented by his bunched-up pants and shoes.*

> CHAD
>
> 'S John Merrick, that's the only thing I can think of, the whole time . . . I am sitting across from the fucking Elephant Man!

CHAD *shivers in disgust as* HOWARD *repositions himself.*

> HOWARD
>
> But she's attractive, though?

> CHAD
>
> Yeah. I guess. . . . yeah, I would say yes.

> HOWARD
>
> Tall?

> CHAD
>
> Kind of. Average . . . but you should see her going at it. Working to put the simplest sounds together . . . I mean, an "a, e, i, o, u, sometimes y" is like the holy grail to this poor wretch! After about fifteen minutes I can't watch any more saliva form, the corner of her mouth, or I'm gonna lose my taco salad, I mean it.

> HOWARD
>
> But was she nice? I mean, you know . . .

> CHAD
>
> Nice? (*beat*) Yeah, sweet, giving, all those things . . .

> HOWARD
>
> That's good.

> CHAD
>
> In fact, one of the kindest people I've ever had spray spit in my face.

The mirror smiles back at CHAD *as he finishes, satisfied with what he sees. He leans back against a sink and waits; there is no movement from the stall.*

CHAD

Are you regrouting in there?

HOWARD

I'm coming, I'm coming . . .

CHAD

Jesus.

HOWARD

So what else?

CHAD

What else is I get her entire family history jotted down on a series of bar napkins, 'cause finally I just asked her to stop talking, if it'd be easier to write . . . (*beat*) So now I'm reading these things all night, playing Twenty Questions . . . family used to live in Germany, the Air Force, lost her hearing at eight or something like that, got some sister doing field work, a PhD— saw her picture, big horsey-looking bitch! Ask to see it if you get the chance—anyway, on and on. 'S endless . . .

HOWARD

Dinner?

CHAD

Yeah, we ate. (*beat*) And guess who doesn't reach for her purse when the check comes?

HOWARD

Huh. Movie?

CHAD

Nah, work night. Besides, starting out easy . . .

HOWARD

So, kiss at the door?

CHAD

Naturally . . .

21

HOWARD

Nice.

CHAD

Just a peck. (*beat*) I'm telling you, she's not bad-looking, over-all, but you watch that mouth working just one time, see those little bubbles forming and popping for a couple seconds, all it takes . . . kiss on the cheek was plenty. (*beat*) But . . . she's perfect for this.

HOWARD

Yeah?

CHAD

Oh . . . better than I expected . . .

HOWARD

Wow. (*beat*) Listen, I'm not checking up or anything, but did you happen to finish those files . . . ?

CHAD *glances quickly about as he fires up a smoke.*

CHAD

Already on your desk. You just need to sign 'em and they'll be outta here by five. (*knocking on the stall again*) Jesus!

HOWARD

Thanks, that's great . . . (*after knock*) I'm coming!

CHAD

No prob'. (*beat*) . . . hey, you're not pussing out on this, are you, Howie?

HOWARD

No, I just don't know if she's really . . .

CHAD

Good. 'Cause I'm not doing this to find a mate, right? Thought we were in this together . . .

HOWARD

No, we are, we are . . .

22

                              CHAD
Okay, then . . . I mean, 's not fun unless we're both in on it.

                             HOWARD
Okay, I'll go down there next week or something, I don't . . .

                              CHAD
Give it a week. (*beat*) Look, Howie, this is not some broken-
winged bluejay I'm talking about here . . . catch her in a couple
'a those big fat lies you like so much, see how you feel about
her then. 'Kay?

                             HOWARD
'Kay . . . (*beat*) You guys doing anything this weekend?

                              CHAD
Yeah.

                             HOWARD
Cool.

                              CHAD
Thought I'd take her to a production of *The Miracle Worker.*

                             HOWARD
What is that, a movie?

                              CHAD
Forget it . . . (*beat*) You gonna come out 'a there or do you want
me to have your calls forwarded?!

                             HOWARD
I'm coming . . . oh, shit!

Change spills out from under the stall and onto the floor. CHAD *collects
the money and waits for* HOWARD. *At the last moment, he pockets several of the coins and hands the rest over the top of the stall as a flush
rings out.*

                              CHAD
I got it, just hurry up! (*as* HOWARD *appears*) Here you go . . .

CUT TO:

INT. COMPANY OFFICE—A LATE NIGHT

CHAD *and* HOWARD *working late.* CHAD *standing in the hallway, practicing his putting while* HOWARD *makes notations on a dry-erase board.* HOWARD *moves to* CHAD *as the ball hits an ashtray a few yards away.*

> HOWARD
>
> Time is it back there . . . you think there's somebody still at the office?

> CHAD
>
> Definitely . . . hey, Howard, what's the difference between a golf ball and a G-spot?

> HOWARD
>
> I dunno . . .

> CHAD
>
> I'll spend twenty minutes looking for a golf ball!

> HOWARD
>
> That's good . . .

> CHAD
> (*laughing*)
> Don't you love that?! A guy downstairs told me that . . .

> HOWARD
>
> No, that's funny . . . (*beat*) 'Least they could do is give us a little office equipment..

> CHAD
>
> No shit . . . we're like Lewis and Clark up here. (*beat*) I'll buzz 'em and let 'em know it's coming . . .

HOWARD *waves and moves off, putting various papers in order.* CHAD *watches him go, then casually moves off to an adjoining room to place a call. He settles into a chair, checks for* HOWARD, *then dials.*

> CHAD
>
> Hello? Yes, I'm calling for Christine, my name's Chad . . . oh, well, thank you. Nice to talk with you, too. No, I wouldn't think of it. No, ma'am, just tell her everybody's really sorry she's

24

down, I guess the flu's been going through the place for weeks now. Oh . . . ohhh! Hope she's up and around soon . . . *(laughs)* Did she get the flowers? Terrific . . . no, I just took a little collection, no big deal. Yes, ma'am. Umm, no, I'd rather not wake her. Just let her know I called. Thanks again . . . you, too. 'Bye.

CUT TO:

FADE IN:

TITLE: WEEK TWO

FADE OUT:

INT. COMPANY TYPING POOL—ONE AFTERNOON

Like cattle at the slaughterhouse—lots of milling, mooing, and tension. The clacking of keyboards, interns darting in and out of hallways, etc.

HOWARD *stands by* CHRISTINE*'s door, an armload of charts with him, casually talking.*

> HOWARD
>
> All I mean is, I just think everything's a business. You know? Whatever you go into—your typing there, my opportunity, umm, directing this project—doesn't matter. Every walk 'a life is an industry, from child care on up and we need to, ahh, take advantage of the situation. Right?

A sound reveals that CHAD *is positioned in the next doorway, listening in.* HOWARD *waves him off as he continues speaking.*

> HOWARD
>
> That's what I think, anyway. Turn that situation to our own advantage. So . . . on a personal level, that's what I'm doing . . . see, I saw you here, as I was passing, thought about it, and figured, what the hell? You know? You gotta take a chance and who knows, this could turn out to be mutually . . . advantageous. This situation, I mean. That's a long-winded way to say I'd like to go out, maybe get a drink sometime. I'm Howard, by the way.

> WOMAN (O.S.)
> I'm free this weekend . . .

25

CHAD*'s ears perk up at this and he dashes over to* HOWARD, *smiling in at the unseen* SECRETARY.

> CHAD
>
> Hi . . . Howard, I need to see you a second . . .

> HOWARD
>
> Ahh . . . I'll be back in a minute.

HOWARD *motions to the typist that he will return and walks off, whispering loudly with* CHAD.

> HOWARD
>
> What're you doing, she saw you!

> CHAD
>
> That's not her.

> HOWARD
>
> What do you mean? . . . .

> CHAD
>
> That's not Christine . . .

> HOWARD
>
> You said the fourth office . . .

> CHAD
>
> I don't know, she's not there. Come on . . . let's go.

> HOWARD
>
> But . . . I asked her out.

> CHAD
>
> Fuck her . . . let's go get a sandwich.

HOWARD *looks back over his shoulder but* CHAD *pulls him down the hall.* HOWARD *shakes his head, laughing at the surreal quality of this encounter.*

CUT TO:

INT. TOWN RESTAURANT—A DIFFERENT EVENING

Midwestern chic but intimate. Lots of plants and privacy. WAITRESSES *mill about with regularity and severity.*

CHRISTINE *looks quite striking and sits listening to* HOWARD, *who is, as always, outfitted in shirt and tie.*

> HOWARD
> And I got out of there, fast as my feet'd go, soon as I turned eighteen. I mean, I bolted, far as I could get . . . My brothers—I've got these two older brothers—they both got their union cards the day after graduation. Not me . . . uh-uh. My dad just couldn't see it . . . thought it was the greatest thing, Chrysler plant, Teamsters and all the rest. Couldn't get enough. (*beat*) The whole Norman Rockwell thing, both my parents . . . church, family, little place in the suburbs and you're in heaven. Right? But I'll tell you, I was ready to apply for colleges in, like, ninth grade! They still think I'm crazy, living in the city.

CHRISTINE, *following along intently, smiles at this and* HOWARD *laughs softly.*

> HOWARD
> Seriously, I just didn't want that at all. And so comes this, ahh . . . (*fabricating*) . . . baseball scholarship. Yeah. But, hey, blew my arm out, sophomore year—and that's why I nabbed

the business degree and got into the "biz." And I like it . . . no big deal. (*beat*) That's me, in a nutshell.

Silence between them for a moment as they both pick at their salads.

> HOWARD
> So tell me . . . (*getting her attention*) . . . tell me about yourself. Are you, umm . . . seeing anyone?

A fork is set down as CHRISTINE *smiles and nods a no; she grabs her purse, searching for a pen while pulling a napkin close.* HOWARD *lays a gentle hand on hers.*

> HOWARD
> Nobody, huh? (*watching her*) No, no, why don't you just say it? You speak fine, really. It's okay.

> CHRISTINE
> Umm . . . I've lived in this town for a few years now. My family moved around a lot, when I was young. My father was in the military. He died from cancer. So we moved here, my mother and I. Her hometown . . . my sister, she lives in Seattle, she goes to school in Seattle. (*beat*) Ahh, I'm not sure what else you might want to know about . . .

A glance around the room on reflex by HOWARD *to see if anyone is watching is almost imperceptible. Almost.* CHRISTINE *stops for a moment but* HOWARD *recovers with a thin smile. An awkward moment.*

> HOWARD
> A sister, huh? That's great . . . (*beat*) Do you have any pictures?

CUT TO:

INT. COMPANY CONFERENCE ROOM—SOME MORNING THAT SAME WEEK

A large glass table that takes up nearly the entire room. Plush chairs all around. A medium-sized skyline out the window.

CHAD *sits in one chair, leafing through a company newsletter. Two or three* COWORKERS, *including* JOHN, *are gathered nearby, halfheartedly studying a series of oversized charts, drinking coffee, etc.*

28

CHAD

Huh. (*chuckling*) I hate this guy. (*to* JOHN) I hate that guy,
too . . . he's a little bastard, you ever met 'im? Jerry something?

JOHN

Nah.

CHAD

Lucky you. (*beat*) Oooh, I hate that dude, right there . . . Craig
or Greg, one 'a those . . . from Pittsburgh. He sucks dick . . .

Another COWORKER *wanders into the room, spots* CHAD *and crosses to
him, sitting on the edge of the table.*

COWORKER 2

Hey . . . how's it going?

CHAD

Good! Haven't seen you since, what?

COWORKER 2

New Jersey. That one seminar . . . (*looking about the room*) Hey,
this is nice . . .

CHAD

Yeah, you believe this shit? When they ship you out here?

COWORKER 2

'Bout ten days ago . . . training on the new dat-com system.

CHAD

Great.

JOHN

Hey . . . (*reading*) . . . I know her. Uuuh, lookit that face!

CHAD

Cunt?

JOHN

Oh yeah . . .

CHAD

Looks it. (*to* COWORKER 2) Anyway . . .

COWORKER 2

Yeah. So, you guys here to finish up that new Computex thing they got going, or . . . ?

CHAD

Yep. In and out, six weeks.

COWORKER 2

Must be nice . . . (*beat*) Hey, that guy you're with, what's his story? Can't get a read on him yet . . .

CHAD

He's cool. First time in charge, so, you know . . . no big deal.

JOHN

Seems okay. So, you two take in any of our nightlife yet?

CHAD

Yeah . . . we ate at Arby's yesterday.

A laugh from the others as CHAD *grins, looking back at the newsletter and leafing through it.*

CHAD

Oooh, man, I despise that dude! Sales rep from Indiana, a major fucker. (*to* COWORKER 2) You gotta remember him . . .

COWORKER 2

Oh yeah . . . Lawrence, don't know his last name. He was up there, too . . .

CHAD

Exactly . . . Lawrence. Now, he's a new breed of fuck, 's like a special strain of fucker! . . . ahh, I hate that prissy little cocksucker . . .

COWORKER 2

No kidding . . . cover your ass, he ends up out here. I mean, literally . . . (*beat*) I gotta head out, we'll catch you later . . .

CHAD

'Kay, good to see you.

COWORKER 2

You, too.

He exits the room and CHAD *returns to his reading.* JOHN *watches* COWORKER 2 *leave, then leans over toward* CHAD *and whispers.*

> JOHN
>
> You like that guy?

> CHAD
>
> Him . . . you kidding me? I hate that prick . . .

They smirk at one another and go back to doing nothing for a moment.

CUT TO:

INT. COMPANY TYPING POOL—SAME TIME

CHRISTINE *knee deep in forms and typing for all she's worth. The whole place is humming today. A* DELIVERY DRIVER *tentatively enters the room, asking questions to* OTHERS *as she goes. After a moment, she approaches* CHRISTINE, *setting a pretty arrangement of flowers on her desk and moving off.*

CHRISTINE *hurriedly pulls the card off the bouquet and looks around, a bit embarrassed. Few coworkers seem genuinely interested, so she takes a few minutes to study the gift. A small "thank you" balloon sticks haphazardly out of the arrangement at an angle. She touches the flowers gingerly, lost in thought. She turns the envelope over and over in her hands.*

CUT TO:

INT. COMPANY CONFERENCE ROOM—SAME TIME

The boys still doing nothing. HOWARD *enters and everyone begins to snap to except for* CHAD, *who glances at* HOWARD *and then goes back to his newsletter.*

> HOWARD
>
> Alright, alright, break time's over . . . I mean, you're all fired. Kidding . . . (*chuckle from* THE GROUP) Good to have you guys up from downstairs, appreciate the help. Sorry about the conditions they've got us in here, repairing the water damage and all . . . Chad calls it—you've all met Chad, right?—He calls it our Jonestown office. (*beat*) . . . well, it was funny when he said it.

CHAD

That's because I said Jamestown. (*laughter*) See?

HOWARD

Right . . . Jamestown. Anyhow, this floor was the biggest thing they could give us, what with the computers and everything we needed, so, we'll make do . . . Okay, what's the best way to do this? Let's break into two teams . . . we'll go one, two, one, two . . .

CHAD

I thought you wanted to do the projection thing . . .

HOWARD

Oh, right. Who's got those graphs? Let's see 'em . . .

CUT TO:

INT. COMPANY XEROX ROOM—A DIFFERENT AFTERNOON

Massive windowless structure, buzzing with bright lights, stacks of paper being shuffled and PEOPLE *lined up to make copies.*

HOWARD *and* COWORKER I *stand at one machine,* HOWARD *fiddling with the buttons in front of him while he chats.*

HOWARD

'S not serious.

COWORKER I

Yeah?

HOWARD

Nah. Just seeing her, you know?

COWORKER I

Right.

HOWARD

Took her to lunch a couple times . . .

COWORKER I

Yeah, and I see your pal there down at her desk, like, every other day. Heard he went to the movies with her . . . (*beat*) Come on, something's going on.

HOWARD

What? It's mostly work, she does some typing for us . . . (*beat*)
Anyway, look, we both just took her out . . . no big deal.

COWORKER I

Sure.

HOWARD

It's not!

COWORKER I

Fine . . . none of my business.

HOWARD *glares at him on this, shaking his head. The* COWORKER *fights a
grin.*

HOWARD

Right. (*beat*) Listen, I know it's probably . . . but I'm telling you
the truth. It's nothing . . .

COWORKER I

Uh-huh.

HOWARD

'S just a coincidence.

COWORKER I

Okay.

HOWARD

She's a nice girl.

COWORKER I

Hey, my hat's off to you. Bigger man than I am.

HOWARD

You don't think she's cute?

COWORKER I

Yeah.

HOWARD

Serious. Got a nice figure . . . ?

COWORKER I

Absolutely.

HOWARD *finishes his copying and the* COWORKER *takes over the machine, placing his work in the feeder.*

> HOWARD
>
> But . . . you wouldn't be caught dead with her. Right?

> COWORKER I
>
> In a company like this? With these guys around? . . . (*beat*) . . . no fucking way.

> HOWARD
> (*to the secretary*)
>
> . . . sorry.

The COWORKER *turns back to the copier as* HOWARD *nods and begins to separate his forms. A blast of light from the copier momentarily obliterates* HOWARD*'s features as he moves aside for a secretary.*

CUT TO:

FADE IN:

TITLE: **WEEK THREE**

FADE OUT:

INT. COMPANY OFFICE—AN EARLY EVENING

HOWARD*'s office, door wide open.* PARTYGOERS *pass by with some regularity, blowing horns and stumbling happily along.* A COWORKER *moves along the passageway, kicking a balloon savagely past.*

HOWARD, *party hat on and a glass of punch on his desk, sits talking on the phone.*

> HOWARD
>
> Hello? Yes, hi, is, umm, Christine home yet? No. Fine, I see.
> (*beat*) No, no message . . . oh, is this one of those phones where
> you can, I mean, is there a readout for her, or, how does . . .
> I'm sorry, obviously that doesn't matter, I'm talking with you.
> I could just tell you, couldn't I? Sorry, just curious . . . it is one,
> okay. Thanks. Umm, just . . . just tell her (*a horn blast*) Be there
> in a second . . . (*back to phone*) no, there's a little office
> thing . . . somebody retiring, I guess. I'm not even sure who . . .

34

Oh, I just wanted to . . . (*a line rings*) Ahh, could you hold on one minute? Thanks . . . (*to phone*) Hello? What?! No, I checked those myself before I had 'em sent out . . .

CUT TO:

EXT. COMPANY OBSERVATION TOWER—SAME TIME

An expanse of concrete that rises up to a decorative lip, then drops off into space. The town beyond. The sun is blazing orange and dropping just behind a building, bathing CHAD *and* CHRISTINE *in a fiery glow as they stand near the edge, pressed together and staring out at the sights.*

> CHAD
>
> It was a nice suggestion, coming out here. I didn't even know this was up here! Thanks for showing me this, Christine . . .

> CHRISTINE
>
> You're welcome.

> CHAD
>
> Yeah. And you got me outta going to some guy's farewell party, so I really appreciate it!

INT. COMPANY OFFICE—SAME TIME

HOWARD *still dealing with the new call. He's getting frustrated.*

> HOWARD
> Well, just check around and call me back, I'm sure they're there. Just dig around. 'Kay. (*clicks over*) Hello? I'm sorry . . . anyhow, I tried to catch her before she left, but I couldn't find her . . . no, no big deal, no, it's . . . uh-huh. Well, it's nice to talk with you . . . Oh, no, my name's Howard. That's alright. Uhh, I just wanted to touch base on a couple office things. No big deal, no. No message. Ahh, goodnight . . .

HOWARD *slowly hangs up, lost in thought.*

CUT TO:

EXT. COMPANY OBSERVATION TOWER—SAME TIME

> CHAD
> So, do you . . . and I don't mean to embarrass you or anything, but . . . (*beat*) . . . forget it.

> CHRISTINE
> No, it's alright. Go ahead . . . (*he falters*) Really . . .

> CHAD
> Well, I was thinking about that drive-in you took me to last week, you know, the movie?

> CHRISTINE
> Yes . . .

> CHAD
> Okay . . . so, when I pulled in there, I just naturally put the speaker on my side because of . . . you know. I just assumed that you wouldn't need it, but . . . am I making any sense?

> CHRISTINE
> Yes.

> CHAD
> No, I'm not, I sound like an idiot!

CHRISTINE

No . . .

CHAD

So, should I have put the thing on . . . ?

CHRISTINE

No, it was fine.

CHAD

You sure? (*beat*) . . . so then, I mean, do you "feel" the sound?
Or, how do you . . . ? Forget it, I'm sorry . . .

CHRISTINE

No, people are curious, it's okay . . . (*beat*) I've seen most of the
movies on TV. I read their lips . . . it helps that their mouths are
fifty feet tall.

CHAD

Yeah . . . (*laughs*) That's terrific . . . I'm sorry for asking, I just . . .

CHRISTINE

It's okay.

CHRISTINE *smiles over at* CHAD *who glances around and then slowly
pulls her close to him and kisses her fully on the mouth. She responds.
They break apart and look at one another.*

CUT TO:

INT. COMPANY OFFICE—SAME TIME

HOWARD *sits for a moment, mulling over the conversation. His hand
finds a noisemaker next to him and he looks at it, twirling it over and
over as the sound of the party rages on nearby.*

CUT TO:

INT. TOWN DELI—A TUESDAY NOON

Quiet eatery downtown. No frills, great food. CUSTOMERS *and* EMPLOY-
EES *are about, ordering, eating, or serving.*

CHAD *sits at the counter, chewing on a dill spear.* HOWARD *sits hunched next to him, examining a sandwich.*

CHAD

'S ham . . . try and get corned beef in this place, I dare ya.

HOWARD

Can't stay long . . . everybody else ordered in. Stuff's piling up.

CHAD

You guys busy up there? I've been working on the main presentation, so I didn't . . .

HOWARD

Oh God, yeah. And you're not gonna believe this . . . that new dude?

CHAD

Which?

HOWARD

That guy, back home . . . Mr. M.B.A., screwed up already. Big time.

38

CHAD

Watch 'em, I told you . . .

HOWARD

Right, well, all that material you faxed to the office . . . suddenly, he can't find it.

CHAD

What?! You're kidding me . . .

HOWARD

No. Found, like, two pages or something . . .

CHAD

Shit. (*beat*) I put the "received" notice on the clipboard. I mean, you can check if you don't . . .

HOWARD

'Course not, I know you did—hand me a napkin, will ya?—just makes us look bad.

CHAD

Why, he's the one who . . . Shoulda checked it when he got it. Dick! . . .

HOWARD

Yeah, but, you know . . . says he didn't notice at first. Now he's messing around, tearing his office up looking for it . . .

CHAD

Serves 'em right . . .

HOWARD

But I'm the one with my thing hanging out of my pants come Monday morning. Hard copy's still on my desk and they're asking why . . . (*beat*) Should've "next dayed" a disk.

CHAD

Well, I did suggest that, but . . .

HOWARD

I know, I know, my fault. (*beat*) Anyhow, we'll get it out today . . . it's just not what I planned.

A bite to the sandwich puts the conversation on hold for a moment. CHAD *sucks on his pickle.*

CHAD

So . . .

HOWARD

How's Christine?

CHAD

Good.

HOWARD

Yeah?

CHAD

Oh yeah . . . (*beat*) You?

HOWARD

Fine. Sent her some flowers . . .

CHAD

Yeah? That's funny . . . me, too.

HOWARD

Hmm.

CHAD

I mean, not running around yet, picking out china patterns . . .

HOWARD

Right.

CHAD

Looking for our "dream cottage". . .

HOWARD

No . . .

CHAD

But it's good. Lot 'a fun, actually . . .

HOWARD

Yeah. I think so, too.

CHAD*'s eyes narrow at this, taking in his friend as he speaks.*

40

CHAD

Uh-huh.

HOWARD

So . . . you're liking her better, then?

CHAD

I don't know, "better." I mean, she's, well, I'm not sure. 'S just
that, every so often, times I'll look over at her and think . . .
"You know, I could almost see myself with this person." Right?
Not when she's talking—'round then you just wanna slip down
a side street, hope no one heard her swallowing her tongue as
she tries to get a sentence out! You know?—but a couple times,
don't know what it'll be, maybe just a look she gives me, this
feeling shoots up the nerve endings as she squeezes my arm,
we're sharing a Slurpee, for God's sake! And, you know, I'll
look over at her, moments like that, and I can see kids and a
Volvo in the garage and all the crap in between. (*beat*) She's
definitely got something . . .

HOWARD

Serious? That's pretty . . .

CHAD

I don't mean exactly that, but, hell, I dunno! I mean, you've
been out with her . . . you get that at all?

HOWARD

Umm . . .

CHAD

'S just every so often. (*beat*) You?

HOWARD

Sure. Kind of.

The ham receives its last rites as HOWARD *looks down and attacks it in
earnest.* CHAD *studies his associate in silence.*

CHAD

Really?

HOWARD

Uh-huh. I mean, yeah . . . (*beat*) She's kinda nice. I mean . . .

41

CHAD

I know. 'S an odd twist, all considered.

HOWARD

'S true.

CHAD

Oh well . . . just see how it goes, I guess.

HOWARD

Uh-huh.

CHAD

'S a serpentine road we travel, this life . . . see where it takes us.

HOWARD

Okay.

CHAD

Sandwich any good?

HOWARD

'S okay. They kinda screw ya on the meat . . .

CHAD

Yep. They sure do.

CUT TO:

INT. COMPANY WINDOWSILL—ANOTHER DAY

Huge pane of glass overlooking the street. A courthouse stands across the way, its American flag waving in the breeze. CHAD *sits near* CO-WORKER 2, *chewing on a Ding-Dong while his associate reads a memo and shakes his head.*

COWORKER 2

You know, I thought you said your friend there was a good guy . . .

CHAD

He is.

COWORKER 2

Yeah, well then how come he's sending me to Bozeman?!

CHAD

Montana?

COWORKER 2

Yes! Fourth of July weekend and I'm going to "big sky" coun-
try . . . some convention he wants me to coordinate the booth
for. That is just . . .

CHAD

Ouch.

COWORKER 2

No, that really stinks, man . . . I had plans.

CHAD

So, tell him. I'm sure he can . . .

COWORKER 2

I already e-mailed 'im. He sent me this back, some "I know the
system best" and that kind 'a crap. Shit . . .

CHAD

Hey, what can I tell ya . . . power corrupts.

COWORKER 2

Yeah, well . . . (*beat*) Ya know the real injustice here? If I could
throw a curve ball, I mean, a really good one—just that, nothing
else, no education, nothing—none of this would matter. Play in
the big leagues for maybe ten years, retire to Oahu.

CHAD

Yep. Life sucks, huh? (*beat*) Hey, listen . . . have fun.

CHAD *fires his best smile off to the coworker, who smirks back and returns
to scouring the note for loopholes while* CHAD *puts his head back on the
glass and stares out the window.*

CUT TO:

EXT. TOWN ZOO—AN EARLY AFTERNOON

*Sleek modern zoo overflowing with plantlife. A few African-style benches
and umbrellas. A handful of visitors about, with* CHRISTINE *standing
nearby, patiently waiting.*

After a moment, HOWARD *hustles onto the scene. He touches* CHRISTINE *on the shoulder, already apologizing as she turns.*

> HOWARD
>
> Sorry. I got held up right when I was leaving. We missed a deadline, I had to ream out a couple guys who were responsible . . . and . . .

> CHRISTINE
>
> I'm sorry . . . "ream"?

> HOWARD
>
> Ream . . . chew out . . . yell?

> CHRISTINE
>
> Oh, I'm sorry.

> HOWARD
>
> That's okay, it all worked out. Anyway . . .

> CHRISTINE
>
> No, I meant for those men . . . *(beat)* I'm sorry they made a mistake. I know your project's important . . . they must've felt terrible.

> HOWARD
>
> Yeah . . . I mean, no, it wasn't that big a deal. I just explained the error to them . . . *(beat)* . . . but it held me up for a bit.

> CHRISTINE
>
> That's okay.

> HOWARD
>
> Thanks . . .

CUT TO:

INT. ZOO CAR—SAME TIME

HOWARD *and* CHRISTINE *crammed into a zebra-striped vehicle that travels along a pulley system.* HOWARD *looks around, playing with the steering wheel.* CHRISTINE *watches, enjoying herself.*

HOWARD

Hey, this is nice . . . (*touching her shoulder*) This is really nice, for a place like this. I mean, a city this size . . .

CHRISTINE

Yes. I like it a lot . . . it's so quiet.

HOWARD *blinks a bit, not knowing how to take this one. He lets it go.*

HOWARD

Right. (*a moment passes*) So, this must be . . . Look, I'm sorry.

CHRISTINE

About what?

HOWARD

What I did, just now. Coming in here with all that "I'm so busy" crap . . .

CHRISTINE

So, you're not busy?

HOWARD

Well, no . . . I mean, yes, I am, but I wasn't . . . I made that up. About disciplining those two guys . . . I just made that up, instead of telling the truth. (*beat*) I ran back to the hotel to change shirts, I wanted to look good. So I was late . . .

CHRISTINE

Oh. That's okay . . .

HOWARD

No, no, it's not alright, I just . . . I guess I'm so used to saying what I think people want to hear that I forget that they might just want the truth sometimes. So, I'm sorry.

CHRISTINE

No, it's alright, really.

HOWARD

Forgive me?

CHRISTINE

Of course . . . (*beat*) Just remember I can't hear you when you're lying . . .

HOWARD

Sure.

CHRISTINE

That's a joke.

HOWARD

Right. (*laughs*) That's good advice, thank you.

CHRISTINE

You're welcome. (*she signs*) "You look good." Oh, you're blushing! I'm glad you made it, late or not . . .

CHRISTINE *shifts her gaze from her date to the exotic foliage that surrounds them.* HOWARD *stares at the young woman beside him.*

CHRISTINE

Oh, look . . . they're beautiful, aren't they?

HOWARD

Yes.

CUT TO:

FADE IN:

TITLE: WEEK FOUR

FADE OUT:

INT. COMPANY OFFICE—ONE DAY THE NEXT WEEK

HOWARD*'s office. Quiet for a moment, the door swung almost completely closed.* HOWARD *sits, feet up, talking on the phone.*

HOWARD

. . . Okay, 'cause I'd like a table facing the water. That's what we want, I mean, I see it in the brochure you sent and we'd really like that . . .

A COWORKER *enters and drops a load of papers on his desk.*

HOWARD

Thanks . . . Oh, oh, I had an idea, if we download the vertical commands off the softpatch, I think we're gonna bypass . . . you know what? Have 'em hold on ten minutes, I'll be down and explain it . . . (*to phone*) Sorry . . . yeah, no, we were thinking of getting in early, dinner, three-thirty, four, something like that, whatever you've got . . .

A SECRETARY *enters and picks up a stack of documents.*

HOWARD

I need those Tuesday . . . (*to the phone*) No, not the reservation, that's for the Fourth. Look, hold on a sec.

The young woman hovers a moment, wanting to ask a question, but HOWARD *waves her off.*

HOWARD

Instructions're on the front, so just . . . look, I gotta take this. (*to the phone*) Excuse me. Uh-huh, uh-huh . . . right. Now, I know it's just a lake, but the view's really stunning this time of year, isn't it? Okay, no, that's fine . . .

CHRISTINE *suddenly enters and drops a sheath of files on his desk. She smiles and mimes a goodbye, but* HOWARD *signals her to wait.*

HOWARD

You have my card number, right, you can just send me confirmation. I gotta go . . . okay. (*hanging up*) Hey, I just got off with . . . sounds like we can go up, a week from Saturday. If you still want to . . . I checked around, it's supposed to be one of the nicest restaurants in the area, so . . .

CHRISTINE

Umm, yes, well probably . . . I just have to check with, ahh . . . I think so. (*beat*) I should get back.

HOWARD

'Kay. Hey, you wanna get lunch? Only if you want to. (*beat*) There's a couple things I'd like to talk to you about . . .

Her watch gets the once over as CHRISTINE *thinks the offer over.*

Well . . . could we do it later this week? Today's bad, lots of reports due, end of the month. You know . . .

HOWARD

Sure, no, just taking a shot . . . you know.

She smiles at him and he puts a hand on her arm as she turns to leave.

HOWARD

Oh, that's a beautiful dress. (*he signs with some difficulty*) "You look good."

CHRISTINE

Thank you.

HOWARD

I mean, you know, that's a nice style for you . . . Probably sounds goofy, coming from a guy like me, but I can tell these things. I really can . . .

She grins and exits with a wave. He watches her go and sits on the edge of his desk. He picks up a file and tries to read. After a second, he drops the document and practices his signing again.

HOWARD
(*signing*)
"You look good. You look good."

CUT TO:

INT. TOWN CAFE—THE SAME AFTERNOON

Same quaint Western eatery as before. A lighted menu above the counter advertises take-out, but a smattering of small tables betrays its pseudo-atmosphere.

CHAD *and* CHRISTINE *sit opposite one another at a table, pretending to study their menus.* CHAD *glances over as he fumbles with his napkin.*

CHAD
Everything okay?

CHRISTINE
Yes.

CHAD
This place's got great barbeque, supposedly. Some of the best in town . . .

CHRISTINE
Yes, it does.

They study the menus in silence for a moment, CHAD *glancing over at* CHRISTINE *on occasion. Finally,* CHAD *looks up and wins* CHRISTINE*'s attention.*

CHAD
Okay, look . . . reason I wanna have lunch, wanna speak to you, 's about us. Just wanna talk, you know?

CHRISTINE *smiles at this and puts down her menu.*

CHAD
Need to say this, get everything out in the open . . . This isn't easy! Hate this part of dating, 's always hard when you start to feel something for a person. Begin to, you know, feel like taking that next step. I mean, you see what I'm trying to say, right? Cards on the table . . .

49

CHRISTINE

Yes . . .

CHAD *scoops up* CHRISTINE*'s hands, looking deeply into her eyes.*

CHAD

You are so beautiful . . . (*beat*) Look, I have to face this, my job ends here in a few weeks . . . and, ahh, I just want you to know, that whatever you do, it's alright with me. Don't care about dates you go on, other guys, you know, and if we're apart for awhile, or . . . well, I just want you to know, whatever happens, I trust you. Okay? (*beat*) Oh, boy. . . . this is really hard . . .

CHAD *looks away as he fumbles with what to say, searching for the right words.* CHRISTINE *doesn't even blink.*

CHAD

I like you. There, I've said it, 's out and I'm gonna eat better now. Don't blush, it's true . . . I look at you and I see good. I see nice, kind, I don't know . . . I'm very happy with you and I want our relationship—you feel it's a relationship, don't you?— I wanna nurture it. And just see us blossom. (*beat*) Aaah! That's what I wanted to say, anyhow. So, let's just enjoy this, 'cause I'm really in the mood for some ribs . . .

CHRISTINE *stares over at* CHAD, *a profound happiness spread across her face. She is about to speak when* HOWARD *walks up to the table, completely unexpected, carrying a take-out salad.* CHRISTINE, CHAD, *and* HOWARD *all seem a bit caught off-guard.* HOWARD *recovers first.*

HOWARD

Hey.

CHAD

Umm, Howard. How are you?!

HOWARD *looks at* CHRISTINE *and she turns away.* CHAD *was right. The big lie.*

CHAD

Chris, you know Howard at all?

50

She falters but HOWARD *steps in and answers quickly.*

> HOWARD
>
> I've, ahh, seen her around . . . hi.

> CHAD
>
> Yeah, Howard's in charge of the project I'm working on; Christine's in with the secretaries, on three.

> HOWARD
>
> Oh, is that right?

> CHAD
>
> This is hilarious . . . suddenly, I see you everywhere! I mean, you know how it is, Christine, Howard and I, we've got the same alma mater—believe this, he graduates a semester ahead of me, now he's my boss!

> HOWARD
>
> It's just on this one project that I'm . . .

> CHAD
>
> No, come on now, don't be modest! They picked you—over me, anyone else—you're it. (*beat*) Got time to sit?

> HOWARD
>
> Ahh . . . no. Need to get back upstairs. (*beat*) Lot of reports due, end of the month. You know . . .

HOWARD *looks straight at* CHRISTINE *on this one; she looks away.*

> CHAD
>
> Too bad. (*grabbing his pager*) Oh, shoot! I gotta take this, I'm sorry, excuse me. I'll be right back . . .

CHAD *smiles briefly and trots off toward the phones.* HOWARD *and* CHRISTINE *are locked in an uncomfortable moment until she whispers at him, looking around as she does.*

> CHRISTINE
>
> I'm so sorry . . .

> HOWARD
>
> 'S okay. (*looking around*) You, ahh, must really like this place . . .

CHRISTINE

No . . . He'd already made plans for . . .

HOWARD

No big deal. Look, ahh, I should . . .

CHRISTINE

Howard . . . (*she signs*) "Forgive me." I still . . .

HOWARD

It's okay.

A last look from HOWARD *is directed at* CHRISTINE *as he softens. He is gone by the time* CHAD *returns.* CHAD *looks about expectantly for his pal.*

CHAD

Where'd Howard go?

CHRISTINE

He said he had to go . . . (*beat*) . . . so, you two . . . I mean, you work together . . . ?

CHAD

Yeah. I do most of the marketing, Howard's more in-house, coordinating all the divisions . . . you knew that, though, right? There's six of us here, brought in from all over for this thing . . .

CHRISTINE

No, I . . . so many people come and go that I . . . didn't know.

CHAD

Well, you do now . . . no big deal. Anyhow, he's a nice guy. Hell of a guy . . . a truly decent person, I think. Yeah. (*beat*) Seriously, you should talk to him sometime . . . Yep, I always liked Howard. (*taking her hand*) Anyhow . . . you wanna get an appetizer, that be alright? I'm so hungry, I could eat forever . . .

CHRISTINE *smiles at* CHAD, *glances once more in the direction that* HOWARD *went, then down at the menu.* CHAD *watches her closely for a long time.* CHRISTINE *continues to scan the pages for food. Finally, she looks back up at* CHAD *just as he turns his gaze down to his menu.*

CUT TO:

EXT. COMPANY OBSERVATION TOWER—ANOTHER AFTERNOON

Same as before, empty except for the boys. Buildings in the distance.

CHAD *leans against a column, sunning himself like a reptile and holding a cup of coffee.* HOWARD *stands at the railing, looking out at the horizon and absently chewing on a sandwich.*

> CHAD
>
> That break room down there's an absolute cesspool!

> HOWARD
>
> Uh-huh . . .

> CHAD
>
> I'm coming out 'a there . . . Howard . . . you were already in the restroom . . . I see three 'a those interns slinking around, like it was some sort 'a summer camp, a food fight or whatever. That just pisses me off! And then they drag their shit upstairs . . .

> HOWARD
>
> Yeah, I'll say something to 'em . . . (*beat*) Boy, it's a great view . . . how'd you find this place?

CHAD

Hmm? Oh, ahh . . . what's her name, Christine. (*beat*) Those fuckers, bunch 'a juvenile fuckers, they leave a place looking like that. Working in a company of men and they still want their mommies wiping their bottoms, every time they go potty.

HOWARD

Yep. I mean, we got two trash cans . . . (*beat*) So, when did you guys come up here . . . ?

CHAD

Exactly. Boy, that just makes me . . . I dunno. (*beat*) We oughta set an example, you know?

HOWARD

You're right. (*beat*) Ahh, got too much to do as it is . . .

CHAD

I know that, Howard. I'm just saying, in theory. In theory something should be done, 'cause back home the place would not look like this. And they should be taught that. (*beat*) I'm just venting a touch, no big deal . . .

HOWARD

Sure.

They smile at one another and go back to their break. HOWARD *checks his watch.*

HOWARD

So, how're things going?

CHAD

Okay. Busy . . .

HOWARD

Yeah?

CHAD

Oh yeah . . . customers, you know. But hitting my deadlines, so . . .

HOWARD

Hey, 'ppreciate that. Love to have this whole thing in place by the holiday . . . (*beat*) . . . you know, I know this is last minute,

54

but—I was thinking maybe you'd fly back over the break and deliver that stuff, make the presentation. If it's alright . . . they wanna know what we've been doing, so it's, umm . . . yeah.

CHAD

I thought you were set to go back on that.

HOWARD

Well, I was, but you know, I just got so much stuff piling up down there . . .

CHAD

Like what, it's the weekend—

HOWARD

Well, you know, things . . .

CHAD
(*offguard*)
Well, why don't we send this John guy? He's up to speed on it . . .

HOWARD

I was gonna, but he doesn't know the city, or the players back there. (*beat*) I think you'd just go a long way toward selling the changes we implemented in the package . . . if you're okay with that. If you're not . . .

CHAD

Sure. I'm salary. There's no such thing as holidays . . . Leave it on your desk, I'll pick it up on Friday.

HOWARD

Terrific. I'll keep an eye on things on this end and we can meet on Monday, review it all . . . 'Preciate it, Chad.

CHAD

'Kay. (*beat*) I was thinking of taking Christine out to, I dunno, ballgame or something, fireworks. Town like this must eat that shit up! But, hey . . .

HOWARD

Yeah. Sorry about that . . . work comes first.

CHAD

Well, you think of something, okay? Keep the heat on . . .

HOWARD

See what I can do. Think I'll be pretty swamped.

CHAD

Yeah, with "things." Well, we still got a little while yet, right?
I mean, 'fore the big finale . . .

HOWARD

Mmm.

CHAD

Listen, 'bout lunch last week. Had no idea, I mean, that you'd
made plans and all. (*beat*) You did, right? Look on your face . . .

HOWARD

No problem.

CHAD

No, seriously. I'm sorry . . .

HOWARD

Don't worry about it.

CHAD

She hadn't told you about it, though, had she? Didn't think
so . . .

HOWARD

We should be careful, though, now that she's seen us . . . I mean,
maybe one of us should pull back.

CHAD

Yeah, maybe so. (*beat*) Who should it be?

HOWARD

Oh, whoever. I just . . . you know what I'm saying? Don't wanna
be too obvious . . .

CHAD

Absolutely . . . or get caught. (*beat*) Things okay, though?
I mean, you're not second-guessing or anything . . .

HOWARD

No. No, I'm still in. (*beat*) You?

CHAD

Yeah.

HOWARD*'s reaction to this is closely studied by* CHAD. HOWARD *shakes his head thoughtfully.*

CHAD

Ever hear from that one girl 'a yours again?

HOWARD

Oh yeah . . .

CHAD

No kidding?

HOWARD

Yep. Calling my mom . . .

CHAD

Ouch.

HOWARD

And I'm getting these messages, my machine, all the time. Nobody says anything . . . but she won't just call me direct. (*beat*) Pisses me off.

CHAD

Give 'em a chance, you know, buy a ring . . .

HOWARD

That bitch.

CHAD

. . . and then back they come, too late. Huh?

HOWARD

Calling my mother! (*beat*) Saw where you got a message the other day, too . . .

CHAD
(*surprised again*)

What?

57

HOWARD

From Suzanne . . .

CHAD

Oh, yeah, yeah . . . believe that?!

HOWARD

I mean, I wasn't snooping . . . saw it stuck to your terminal one
time last week. Secretary must've . . .

CHAD

Right. No, she, umm . . . tracked me down here somehow.
Never called back again, but, see, that's what I'm talking
about! . . .

HOWARD

I know.

CHAD

Just when you start feeling sorry for somebody, like Christine
there . . . they come back and kick you straight in the teeth.
(*beat*) Women. Nice ones, the most frigid of the race, doesn't
matter in the end . . . inside, they're all the same. Meat, and
gristle, and hatred. Just simmering . . . and I, for one, have had
it with their shit. Know what I mean? Makes me just wanna . . .
something.

HOWARD

Sure.

On this, CHAD *finishes his coffee with a final gulp.* HOWARD *surveys his
limp sandwich.*

CUT TO:

FADE IN:

TITLE: WEEK FIVE

FADE OUT:

INT. TOWN HOTEL ROOM—EARLY AFTERNOON ON A TUESDAY

Elegant suite overlooking the city. Ornate, romantic. Crisp linens.

58

CHRISTINE *lies in bed, staring off into space as the warm pale of the afternoon spills through a window. After a moment,* CHAD *enters, pulling on his shirt and buttoning it. He crosses to the bed and sits on the edge of the mattress, kissing* CHRISTINE *lightly.*

CHRISTINE

It was fun sneaking away from work . . . I've never done that before. (*beat*) I like your room.

CHAD

You do, huh? . . . (*beat*) God, I'm just so . . . taken. You know? Me, I'm taken with you, and . . . I'm done, I promise. Probably sound pretty stupid . . .

She scoots across the bed to him, folding both arms over his shoulders. He returns the favor.

CHRISTINE

You sound wonderful to me.

CHAD

You're so fragile . . . I can't imagine ever not having you here, feel so perfect in my arms. (*beat*) I can't believe I'm not gonna be here for the Fourth! I really wanted to . . .

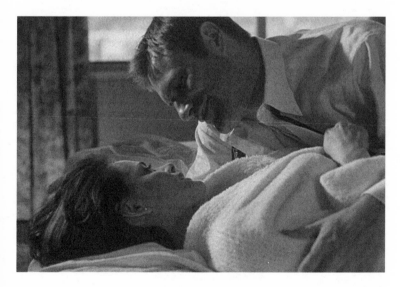

59

CHRISTINE

I know. It's work, you can't help it.

CHAD

Yeah. Still stinks . . . (*beat*) We should get back to work . . .

CHRISTINE *shakes her head no and smiles. A moment passes while she studies* CHAD.

CHRISTINE

Chad . . . do you love me? (*beat*) I'm sorry . . .

CHAD

No, no, no, no, no . . . what?

CHRISTINE

I think I love you. (*beat*) And I just wanted to know if . . .

CHAD

Yes. Yes, I do.

THE LOVERS *embrace, falling back and kissing with increasing intensity. The sun blazes in as the room heats up.*

CUT TO:

INT. TOWN JEWELRY STORE—JUST BEFORE THE WEEKEND

Small shop wedged in a downtown block. Elegant, traditional. A few PATRONS *gaze into glass cases or deal with* SALESPEOPLE.

HOWARD *stands at a counter on his lunch break, talking to an older* EMPLOYEE *who studies a ring beneath a magnifying glass.*

HOWARD

No, I'm not asking for an estimate. Don't want to sell it, alright? Just like to get the thing cleaned. Maybe have you check that back post. Feels loose . . . I mean, I know it is . . . ended up practically ripping it off a girl's finger! Didn't want it, first time, few weeks later I couldn't get her to give it back . . . "Just want to try it on," ended up wrestling on the floor one night. Me pulling on her hand, she's screaming, neighbors at the door. What a mess . . . (*beat*) And that's why it's bent, a little . . . plus, been carrying it in my wallet for about four months.

HOWARD *stops talking for a moment while the* EMPLOYEE *holds the ring up to the light, examining the posts. He steals a glance at* HOWARD *when he's not looking.*

> HOWARD
> So . . . just polish it up. Make sure it's all okay . . . (*beat*) I'm gonna take a look at your china.

CUT TO:

INT. COMPANY OFFICE—SAME TIME

HOWARD'*s office. The blinds are standing open, only a lamp on although it's still daytime.* CHAD *sits at the desk, alternating between taking bites from a sandwich and filling his briefcase with papers.*

A young black INTERN *stands in front of him, listening to him speak between mouthfuls.*

> CHAD
> 'S a disgrace. That's what it is . . .

> INTERN
> I know.

> CHAD
> I mean, you guys are privileged, you see that, right?

> INTERN
> Sure.

> CHAD
> No, not "sure" and out the door, give me the finger you get halfway down the hall . . . want you to know a thing because it's true. Not because some dude—this time me but could be anybody—because some man says it's right. (*beat*) You know, I could've held back on this, just blown it off 'cause I've got a flight to catch tomorrow, let you figure out life all on your little lonesome, but I think I would've been doing you a disservice. I really do . . . so—and I'm not bullshitting you here—cherish this.

61

His sandwich is set down for emphasis as CHAD *wipes his mouth daintily with a napkin. The* INTERN *shuffles a bit, looking over at a large wall clock.*

> CHAD
>
> Look, all I wanna say is, you boys are sitting in the driver's seat, make whatever you want happen happen. 'S that easy, you're in with this company . . . but you're screwing around, chasing each other in the break room, hanging out with a bunch of guys from shipping . . . where is your head, huh?

THE YOUNG MAN *shrugs and* CHAD *smiles at this, shaking his head wearily.*

> CHAD
>
> Offering you a chance here . . . Keith, right?

> INTERN
>
> Yeah. 'Kef.'

> CHAD
>
> Hmm? (*beat*) Keith or Kef?

> INTERN
>
> Kef.

CHAD

Which?

INTERN

"Keith . . ."

CHAD

Well, you oughta know . . . (*a* COWORKER *knocks*) Yeah, Howard'll be back in about an hour . . . I'll take 'em. Thanks.

CHAD *sees the employee out and then crosses to the blinds, snapping them closed one by one.*

CHAD

I'm just rolling out the opportunity for you to hang with the money people. Don't screw this up, Keith . . . I look at you guys sometimes, interns we're given on a project, I mean, I'll wonder to myself, I will, "He got the balls for this?" Right? I can't help but think it . . .

INTERN

I do.

CHAD

Yeah?

INTERN

Yes . . . ax anybody.

CHAD *lets the moment hang for a bit while he sips a cup of coffee.*

CHAD

Lemme give you a professional tip . . . the word is "ask." Okay? (*beat*) You want a job like mine, one day, sitting back and part of a show such as this one? The ring is just dangling right there, you've come this far, just gotta grab for it . . . but you need the big brass ones for the task. (*beat*) Now . . . you say you've got 'em?

INTERN

Yeah.

CHAD

Enough to handle a pressure cooker like this?

                              INTERN

    Uh-huh . . .

CHAD *toys with the sandwich as he takes in this info.*

                              CHAD

    Fine. (*takes a bite*) Let's see 'em, then . . .

                             INTERN

    Huh?

                              CHAD

    These clankers of yours, let's see what you got.

CHAD *smiles and rises, crossing to the door. He snaps the lock into place
and moves to a couch, sitting down. The* INTERN *turns to face him,
uncertain about what is happening.*

                              CHAD

    Not a homo, Keith, gonna leap across the table at you . . . just
    wanna be sure you got what it takes. (*beat*) They asked me to
    recommend someone for the management trainee program
    before I go. So . . . you decide.

                             INTERN

    Wait, wait, wait, wait, wait . . .

                              CHAD

    Show me your balls.

                             INTERN

    I don't . . .

                              CHAD

    Listen, you got a pair, the kind that men are carrying around,
    practically wear 'em on your sleeve! 'S what business is all
    about . . . who's sporting the nastiest sac of venom. And who
    is willing to use it. (*beat*) Don't be embarrassed.

The INTERN *looks at* CHAD *again, then slowly undoes his fly. His pants
slip down onto his thighs and the boy pulls his underwear down a bit.*
CHAD *indicates lower, and the briefs move a touch more.* CHAD *leans
forward, inspecting the young man's scrotum.*

CHAD

Alright, great . . . (*beat*) You feel okay?

CHAD *rises from the couch, patting the* INTERN *on the shoulder as he crosses back to the desk. The* INTERN *quickly pulls up his pants and refastens them while nodding a quick yes.* CHAD *sits and begins writing on a legal pad. He doesn't look up again.*

CHAD

Good. (*beat*) Then get me a cup 'a coffee before you take off, alright? Black's fine . . .

The INTERN *starts to say something, stops, then moves to the door. He fumbles with the lock and exits quickly. After he is gone,* CHAD *turns to the window and snaps open the blinds, light spilling in as the razor-sharp CLAP! of the metal shades rings out. He lights up a cigarette.*

CUT TO:

INT. RESORT RESTAURANT—SATURDAY AFTERNOON

Fashionably rustic. Wood paneling and homey furnishings. Large windows overlooking the water dominate the room. A number of GUESTS *and* EMPLOYEES *move or sit about.*

CHRISTINE *sits at a table with* HOWARD, *both of them picking at rolls and trying to enjoy the view. Rain comes down in buckets. Beneath the table,* HOWARD *plays with the ring as he and* CHRISTINE *catch each other's glance.*

HOWARD

Hey. I was thinking later we'd go for a walk by the lake. Supposed to be great fireworks, later . . .

HOWARD *studies* CHRISTINE *as he reaches over and touches her hand. A brief smile appears on her lips.*

HOWARD

Listen, is everything okay?

CHRISTINE

Yes.

HOWARD

I mean, this place, the meal . . . 's okay?

CHRISTINE

Sure.

HOWARD

Good. (*beat*) 'Cause I want to tell you . . . wanted you to know . . .

CHRISTINE

Howard . . .

HOWARD

Maybe this isn't the perfect time, but—I care about you, Christine. I just want you to know, I just like you a lot.

CHRISTINE

Howard, I need to. . . .

HOWARD

I mean . . . I just don't wanna lose this and . . . so I . . . you know, we'd give up certain things. Freedoms. And distance'd be a problem for awhile but I could get a transfer . . . but I need you. Come to realize that and I'm telling you. (*signing*) "I need you." Taught myself that. "I need you . . ."

CHRISTINE

Howard, please listen to me. (*beat*) I've let this go too far . . .

Silence from her. CHRISTINE *begins to speak several times before any words come out.* HOWARD *nervously fingers the diamond.*

HOWARD

Too far?

CHRISTINE

Yes . . . I should've told you before, but I . . . (*beat*) . . . I love someone else.

HOWARD

I'm sorry?

CHRISTINE

I made a mistake. I mean, I like you, I do . . .

66

HOWARD

Christine . . .

CHRISTINE

And you made all these plans, I didn't want you to feel that . . .
but it was wrong for me to come here.

HOWARD

No, I mean . . . no. This is our trip. We worked this out . . .
's not just me. I mean, we've been going out, we've . . . been
dating, you, what're you . . . ?

CHRISTINE

'S the man you met, saw me with at lunch. Chad. Your friend
from school . . . Chad and I, that's who I love.

HOWARD

Ohh . . .

CHRISTINE

I know it's a surprise . . . for me, too.

Reality sinks in like a knife as HOWARD *slowly realizes the ugly truth.
The ring disappears back into a khaki pocket as a* WAITRESS *drops off
a round of coffees.*

HOWARD

Chad.

CHRISTINE

Yes. (*beat*) He likes you a lot . . .

HOWARD

Yeah?

CHRISTINE

Yes, he does . . .

HOWARD

Uh-huh.

CHRISTINE

I'm sorry.

HOWARD

Right.

CHRISTINE

No, I am . . .

HOWARD

Sure . . .

CHRISTINE

Howard . . .

HOWARD

Okay, you're sorry. Terrific . . .

CHRISTINE

I didn't mean for this to . . . it's all my fault.

HOWARD

No . . .

CHRISTINE

I shouldn't have dated both of you . . .

HOWARD

No, no.

CHRISTINE

No . . . you both should've known about this. (*beat*) When you don't date for awhile, you . . . wonder if you're attractive or interesting to someone. You let things get out of hand, first chance you get. That's what I did . . .

HOWARD

I see.

CHRISTINE

It's just . . . when I saw you at lunch that day, and you were saying things like "friends," and you went to school together?! I couldn't believe it . . . I had no idea that the two of you . . . It was fate. I didn't want to hurt anyone and I'm so sorry. (*beat*) . . . it was a lot of fun. Really.

HOWARD *stands suddenly, gesturing for a check and putting his napkin on the table. He points at* CHRISTINE *and speaks hastily.*

> HOWARD
>
> This is, ahh . . . look, let's get outta here, huh? Just get your stuff together and I'll . . . (*beat*) I'll pay the check. I'm sorry . . . yeah.

He turns and exits the room without a smile. CHRISTINE *remains seated.*

CUT TO:

INT. RENTAL CAR—A BIT LATER

Light rain on the windshield. The glare of lights passing. HOWARD *is at the wheel, eyes squinting against the difficult driving.* CHRISTINE *withdrawn into one corner. No one speaking.*

The steering wheel receives a hard right as HOWARD *suddenly cuts over two lanes and pulls off into a rest stop. A horn blasts behind them.* CHRISTINE, *justifiably frightened, looks over at* HOWARD, *who stares straight ahead for a moment.*

> CHRISTINE
>
> Howard! What's wrong . . . ?! (*beat*) What?

> HOWARD
>
> I can't . . . (*beat*) We did.

> CHRISTINE
>
> What?

> HOWARD
>
> We did know, Christine.

> CHRISTINE
>
> Howard, I don't know what you're talking about . . .

> HOWARD
>
> This is priceless . . . You went out with me, dated me, had fun with me but you went to bed with him—don't say anything, I can tell—and I'm sitting here, some asshole who cares about you . . . and you're in love with him!

69

CHRISTINE

Please don't do this . . .

HOWARD

No! I mean, are you so desperate, can't see a yard in front of
you? Huh?! Chad?!! He doesn't like you . . . he loathes you!!
He detests you and your pathetic "retard" voice . . . 's what he
calls it.

Her eyes begin to well up; HOWARD *isn't playing fair.*

CHRISTINE

No . . .

HOWARD

Christine, you bought that shit, "See each other at parties?"
Huh?! 'S my friend, okay, we hang out back home . . . (*beat*)
Better wake up . . . you were used. It's a game, to Chad it was
a game and he found you . . . so perfect. "She's deaf!" he said,
that was the thing . . . (*beat*) Not love you. Not flowers and the
feelings I have for you inside . . . no, it's meant to be a sport
and fun to watch you fall apart . . . and I'm telling you . . .

He moves to touch her, reaching out. Although tied down by her seatbelt, CHRISTINE *fights to keep her distance as* HOWARD *strains against the webbing of his own.*

CHRISTINE

Stop it! . . .

HOWARD

Christine, we did this thing and I'm sorry, but I can't change it . . . I can't! Because it's true . . .

CHRISTINE

No!! Chad would never do that . . .

HOWARD

Why are you trusting him?! Huh?! Look at me, what'd I ever do to you? Kindness, courtesy . . . I mean, what's the matter with you, can't you see . . . I'm the good guy! I'm the good person here!!!

A tear trickles down her cheek and HOWARD *reaches out for it. She turns away first and brushes at it.*

HOWARD

I can't alter what's happened and I'm a fuck and a bastard and the rest on your list but I'm here . . . I'm here and I'm telling you I love you. (*pulls out the ring*) Here, please, it's for you . . . here . . . please, just take this, it's for you . . . it's not a game to me anymore, it's not a game . . . take it. Please, just take it, come on. . . .

HOWARD *reaches out to her again but she slaps his hand away repeatedly. He doesn't fight back. In an instant* CHRISTINE *grabs for the door handle but* HOWARD *is a tad quicker. He slams the lock down with a free hand and lands nearly on top of her, holding her down. He tries to kiss her as she screams at him. He fails.*

CHRISTINE

Get away from me!!

71

HOWARD
(*exploding*)
You are fucking handicapped!! You think you can choose, men
falling at your feet?!!

Suddenly HOWARD *grabs her jaw in his hand, holding her as she fights
to pull away.*

HOWARD
You wanna call Chad?! (*points to a pay phone*) Huh?! Give him
a call, ask about our little contest?!!

CHRISTINE *gives up and begins to sob.* HOWARD *moves off her and slides
back into the driver's seat.*

HOWARD
Christine . . . (*beat*) Fine. No, I'm lying, don't believe me. Go
ahead, go to 'im. Curl up in a little bundle on his lap, suck on
his sour tongue, I don't . . . (*beat*) I hope you're very happy.

HOWARD *slams the car into gear and pulls off, the taillights finally trail-
ing off into the darkness.*

CUT TO:

FADE IN:

TITLE: WEEK SIX

FADE OUT:

INT. COMPANY MEN'S ROOM—TUESDAY MORNING

Back at the palace. COWORKERS *move about the room, in and out of
various stalls, combing hair, etc.*

CHAD *stands at a urinal, in no particular hurry and staring off into
space. After a moment* HOWARD *enters, sees* CHAD, *almost turns away
but finally joins his friend at the porcelain.*

CHAD
Hey.

HOWARD
Yeah.

CHAD

'S up?

HOWARD

Nothing. Little outta joint, that's all.

CHAD

Yeah. Listen, didn't make it in yesterday, but you heard what happened, right?

HOWARD

Part of it. Had, like, ten messages on my voice-mail when I got in yesterday . . .

CHAD

Yeah, I tried your beeper, too, but . . . just couldn't find you.

HOWARD

Umm. I must've turned it off or . . . so, what happened?

The deed is done and the boys head over to the sinks, zipping up on the way.

CHAD

Oh nothing . . . just had about a dozen guys standing there, holiday weekend, and four pages are so light I can't read 'em.

HOWARD

What?

CHAD

Not even the access codes! . . . The old man's looking like I personally fucked up his tee shot on eighteen. (*beat*) He was not pleased . . .

HOWARD

Great. And . . . ?

CHAD

Luckily I got ahold of that one dude from downstairs . . . and he drove in and dug around. Found enough for me to get into the system and I bullshitted the rest . . . covered us for now.

HOWARD

I checked those copies myself!

CHAD

Well, all I know's I took what you left for me. Opened the envelope right in front of 'em . . .

HOWARD

I'm sure I did! Shit!! . . . (*beat*) They want me back for a meeting on Thursday . . . (*laughs*) Things are cool, I guess, but . . . you know.

CHAD

Yeah, no big deal. So you fucked up their Sunday brunch, how bad can that be? (*beat*) We're outta here next Wednesday, anyhow, the thing's done . . .

HOWARD

Right. Well, Friday for me, but . . . (*beat*) It just looks . . . I'll see you.

CHAD

Anyway, how 'bout you . . . good weekend? I mean, considering . . .

HOWARD

Fine.

CHAD

Mmm. See Christine?

HOWARD

Uh-huh.

CHAD

Really? What'd you guys do . . . ?

HOWARD

Just a drive. Some dinner.

CHAD

A drive . . . that's nice. Quaint. Little *Magnificent Ambersons*
thing going on there or . . . ?

HOWARD

Yeah, whatever.

CHAD

Yep, nothing like a drive, you need some time to yourselves . . .
(*beat*) . . . well, see you later, okay?

HOWARD

Yeah, so long.

CHAD *is gone and* HOWARD *turns to wash his hands, but he simply stares
into the mirror for an excruciatingly long time.*

CUT TO:

INT. COMPANY PARKING GARAGE—FRIDAY IN THE A.M.

Expanse of concrete and blacktop. HOWARD *sitting in the rental and
staring out the window. A familiar* COWORKER *beside him at the wheel,
sipping coffee and acting patient.*

HOWARD

No . . . I just don't like what's going on here, that's all. I've been
with the company six years, not taking me off a job without
some sort 'a fight. Gimme a courtesy call, you know? Couple
little glitches and I'm suddenly working on customer support?!
No, uh-uh . . . that is bullshit, okay? (*beat*) I don't care if Chad's
got more background in software, they should've thought
'a that before they . . . I get a demotion, blink of an eye, and
someone's gonna answer. Right?

COWORKER I

What're you talking about?

HOWARD

Nothing, I'm just babbling . . .

COWORKER I

Geez. (*beat*) Glad it's not like that around here . . .

HOWARD

No kidding. (*beat*) Turn my back, go away for the weekend,
and the earth does a nosedive on me! Work, my old girlfriend—
that's a story in itself! Won't speak to me but she's calling my
parents—I mean . . . what the hell has happened here? I used
to be, like, this adjusted person . . .

CUT TO:

INT. TOWN HOTEL ROOM—AN EVENING THE NEXT WEEK

*Similar room, same situation. The lovers on the bed, intertwined. Moon-
light in through the window.*

CHAD *reaches over, kissing* CHRISTINE *and moving to take her blouse off.*
CHRISTINE *watches him, finally touching him and speaking out.*

CHRISTINE

Chad.

CHAD

Hmm?

CHRISTINE

I don't . . .

CHAD

No? That's okay . . .

CHRISTINE

No, I don't mean that . . . I need to . . .

CHAD

What? (*beat*) I'm sorry I haven't been able to see you for a few days, you know, we're finishing things up right now and it's been busy . . . anyway, I did want to, I left a message with your mom . . .

CHRISTINE

I know.

CHAD

Good. Come here. (*holding her*) We are going to see each other again. I promise you . . . (*kissing her*) I know this is hard . . .

CHRISTINE

Do you love me?

77

CHAD

Yes. Just like yesterday . . .

CHRISTINE

Do you really love me?

CHAD

Of course.

CHRISTINE

Oh.

CHAD *studies her a moment, pulling her close.*

CHAD

'S the matter? Quiet all night . . .

CHRISTINE

I know.

CHAD

What?

CHRISTINE

Chad . . .

CHAD

No, seriously, what? Have I done something . . . ?

CHRISTINE

I know what's going on.

A blank expression on CHAD*'s face, only a flickering of the pupils betrays him. He's been caught off-guard and he's fighting to regain his footing.*

CHAD

What? . . . what? I don't . . . oh. (*beat*) You mean Howard. You and Howard, right, you went out with him a couple times or whatever . . . and when I was gone.

CHRISTINE

Yes.

CHAD

Yeah, he told me about your trip. I drove him to the airport and he told me. I was gonna say something, but . . . I mean . . .

(*beat*) Listen, doesn't matter . . . we talked about seeing other people, right?

Now CHRISTINE *is confused as she stares at* CHAD. *She doesn't really want the truth but she digs in one last time anyway.*

CHRISTINE

Yes, but . . . (*beat*) Chad, I know . . .

CHAD

I told you it's okay, I still . . . I just figured that you were probably embarrassed. That's why you didn't say anything.

CHRISTINE

No, about what you're doing.

CHAD

Wait, now you're confusing me, 'cause I don't know what you're talking about . . .

CHRISTINE

What you two are doing to me. Howard told me . . .

CHAD

Christine, look . . . this is silly, because I don't know . . .

CHAD *tries to gather himself but* CHRISTINE *is burning a hole right through him.*

CHRISTINE

The game, the game! You two were playing a game with me!! Right? (*beat*) Chad? Are you . . . are you playing a game with me . . . ? Please tell me . . .

He isn't giving an inch and she studies him, praying that his uncertainty means she's wrong. CHAD *puts a hand over his mouth and shakes his head, not clear about what she could mean.*

CHAD

Howard told you, huh? Well, well . . . (*beat*) . . . alright, listen, don't say anything for a second, lemme explain, okay? . . . shit. Christine, it wasn't a game, but . . . we both noticed you. And we'd—please try and understand—yes, it turned into sort of a contest because we both wanted to . . . (*smiling*) Forget it . . .

79

I was gonna try and let you down easy, but I can't keep a
straight face . . . so, fuck it. Surprise . . .

CHRISTINE *looks at* CHAD *in horror. She starts to move away but* CHAD
grabs her firmly by the jaw.

> CHAD
>
> So . . . how does it feel? I mean, right now. This instant. How
> do you feel inside, knowing what you know? (*beat*) Tell me . . .

Silence as CHRISTINE *stares at him. Suddenly, she slaps him soundly
across the face and he lets go.*

> CHAD
>
> 'S that all? It only hurts that much? (*beat*) I guess I can go,
> then, huh? The deed's done . . .

CHAD *immediately rises from the bed and crosses to gather his jacket.
As he is leaving* CHRISTINE *slowly curls up on the comforter, paralyzed
by this revelation. After a moment, she begins to wail without any sound
being produced as the tears flow.*

CUT TO:

FADE IN:

TITLE: WEEKS LATER

FADE OUT:

INT. CHAD'S TOWNHOUSE LIVING ROOM—WEEKS LATER

*An unfinished living room. Plastic and sheets over most of the furniture.
Fresh paint.*

CHAD *sits hunched on a loveseat, watching television and laughing
quietly to himself. A Kool dangles from his lips. There is no sound from
the TV. After a moment, there is a knock at the door.* CHAD *sits a second,
considering, then rises and goes to the hallway.*

> CHAD
>
> Who is it?

> HOWARD
>
> It's me.

HOWARD *is let into the room. He is soaking wet and standing in his over-coat. Pellets of water spill from his jacket to the wood floor below, beading up in small pools as he wanders about the entryway.* CHAD *stands back and observes his friend and his parquet with equal concern.*

CHAD

Hey.

HOWARD

Hi.

CHAD

'S going on? It's almost one, Howie . . . (*beat*) at my home.

HOWARD *nods without answering, moving into the living room and sit-ting without asking.*

HOWARD

Yeah. Sorry . . . couldn't sleep.

CHAD

Oh.

HOWARD

'S nice. (*taking in the room*) Really. 'S a little smaller than your last place . . .

CHAD

Yeah, but it's a great old building. Plus the park . . .

HOWARD

Right. No, it's terrific . . .

CHAD

Still doing a little touch-up, but . . .

HOWARD

Yeah. Looks like . . . (*pointing to one corner*) you got a new frame there for the "Gigolo" right? Looks good . . . (*beat*) Almost got, and I mean this the right way . . . a woman's touch.

CHAD *shrugs, not fully comprehending the meaning of all this.*

CHAD

Thank you, Howard . . .

81

HOWARD

Sure. (*silence*) . . .

CHAD

So . . . what is it?

HOWARD

I don't know . . . I mean . . . shit. (*fidgeting*) Last couple days,
I'm getting maybe three hours a night. I cannot eat, couldn't
keep rice pudding down yesterday afternoon . . . bought some
at lunch and I threw up, like, thirty minutes later.

CHAD

'S fascinating, Howie.

HOWARD

Just illustrating my point.

CHAD

Fine.

HOWARD

I'm sick, Chad. I am dying here . . . I mean, this whole . . .
fuck.

CHAD

I know, I know, and it puts me in a pretty shitty position, too,
you know? I mean, I didn't ask for this thing . . . and then they
move you downstairs with that new dude on three! I mean,
Goddamn . . . (*beat*) Told you to watch out.

HOWARD

No, Chad, look . . .

CHAD

Whaddya want, that corner office? I can say something if that's
what you're . . .

HOWARD

. . . it's Christine.

CHAD

. . . oh.

HOWARD

I'm here, gotta talk . . . because of her.

CHAD

Mmm. (*beat*) You did it, right?

HOWARD

What?

CHAD

Told her.

HOWARD

Yeah. It just sorta . . .

CHAD

Uh-huh. Kinda caught me off-guard, you know? You might've said something to me first. (*beat*) Thought it was an unwritten that we'd keep the mechanics of it to ourselves, but . . .

HOWARD *starts to says something but simply shrugs.* CHAD *pursues this.*

CHAD

. . . so, everything? She said you told her everything.

HOWARD

Yes.

CHAD

And?

HOWARD

Ahh, come on, Chad . . .

CHAD

Just curious, Howard. I think I'm allowed that . . . (*beat*) So, how'd it feel? Hmm?

HOWARD

Lousy, okay?! Jesus . . . she just fell apart.

CHAD

You told her that I . . .

83

HOWARD

Yes! I told her and I'm watching this . . . oh, God, I can't believe I . . .

CHAD

Man . . . wish I'd 've been there.

HOWARD

I mean, I have never done anything like that! . . .

CHAD

I did it short. Over in a second. Left her sobbing, the hotel room, and then I walked over to Pizza Hut. (*beat*) Your hotel room, actually . . .

HOWARD

What?

CHAD

See, I knew you were gonna be late, wrapping stuff up so I took the liberty. Got a maid to open up and . . . well, I did the same thing when I first fucked her. (*beat*) . . . I thought that you might find her there. Anyway . . .

CHAD *starts to get up but* HOWARD *pulls him back down, holding onto his arm.*

HOWARD

Chad!

CHAD

What?

HOWARD

I'm trying to tell you I'm in love with her! (*beat*) Jesus Christ . . .

CHAD

. . . Oh.

HOWARD

You know, 's a game and all, okay, 's funny! First to agree with you, but . . . shit. (*beat*) I just . . .

A finger suddenly goes to CHAD*'s lips as he studies his friend. He beckons* HOWARD *to follow and they cross to a hall and exit. The camera holds* *on this until* HOWARD *and* CHAD *reenter the main living space and sit in silence.* CHAD *picks up the channel changer and flicks through a few stations as* HOWARD *stares at him.*

HOWARD

When did she get here?

CHAD

What do you mean?

HOWARD

What do you mean, what do I mean? . . . that is Suzanne, right?

CHAD

Sure.

HOWARD

And she's sleeping there, middle of your king-size . . . so, I mean, what the hell? (*beat*) I mean, when'd she crawl back?

CHAD

Let's see . . . this is what, Friday?

HOWARD

Yeah.

CHAD

So, Friday, three days'd be . . . ahh, never.

HOWARD

Huh?

CHAD

She never left, Howie. (*beat*) You're getting all weepy on me here and I gotta get some sleep 'cause we're going to the beach in the morning. So, I'm letting you in on the truth . . . She never left, she's always been right here . . .

HOWARD

Huh? . . . whaaa? (*beat*) Then, I mean . . . Then why, Chad? Why?

CHAD

Because I could . . .

85

The truth spills down all over HOWARD *now, landing on his shoulders like Hermes tumbling from Mt. Olympus.*

> HOWARD

Oh my god . . .

He stands, trying to form words, but nothing comes out. He moves to CHAD, *trying to strike out at him but not finding the strength for even this. He turns for the door but stops as* CHAD *unloads a last buckshot of words with both barrels.* HOWARD *nearly staggers over this one.*

> CHAD

So, how's it feel, Howie? How's it feel to really hurt someone?

> HOWARD

Oh my god.

He stumbles to the door. He looks back briefly, his mouth trying to work, but he simply wanders off into the night. CHAD *slowly swings the door closed as he calls out.*

> CHAD

See you Monday.

CUT TO:

INT. TOWNHOUSE STAIRWELL—SAME TIME

HOWARD *moving quickly down a flight of marble stairs, clutching the brass railing as he goes. Suddenly, he sags into a corner, looks wildly about, and then purges. The vomit flows and flows.*

CUT TO:

CHAD'S TOWNHOUSE BEDROOM—NOT LONG AFTER THIS

SUZANNE *on her back, purring away in dreamland. Young, beautiful, a mane of blonde hair. After a moment,* CHAD *slips into bed next to her, eyes open and staring up quietly at the ceiling. Her eyes flutter open at the movement and she moves to him, slipping a comforting arm across his chest.* CHAD *smiles.*

86

SUZANNE

Time is it?

CHAD

Mmmm . . . (*kissing her head*) 'S around one.

SUZANNE

Not tired?

CHAD

Nah. Just finishing a program . . . (*another kiss*) You smell nice.

SUZANNE

Thanks . . . (*beat*) Did I hear somebody come over? Thought
I did, but I was . . .

CHAD

Nah, I was just talking to myself.

SUZANNE

Really?

CHAD

Uh-huh. I was working on my presentation earlier, but that's
all . . .

SUZANNE

'Kay.

CHAD

I mean, you know me, right?

SUZANNE

I sure do . . .

CHAD

I get working, and I can sound like practically anybody.

*She begins to kiss him, first on the face but continuing on, down and
down.* CHAD *doesn't stop her, instead caressing the top of her head as he
stares off, smiling.*

87

CUT TO:

INT. COMMUTER AIRPLANE—THE NEXT MORNING

An express connection from one city to the next. Populated mostly with early-morning BUSINESS TRAVELERS *and* OLD FOLKS. *One* FLIGHT ATTENDANT *makes her way along, dishing out coffee.*

HOWARD *sleeps nearby, bathed in brightness as he slumps in one corner. He wears the same clothes and has his coat rolled up as a makeshift pillow. He wakes sharply and watches the woman walk away, a smile to him over her shoulder while she continues on.* HOWARD *returns it but without meaning it. He glances at his window and pulls the shade down, flooding himself with darkness.*

CUT TO:

INT. TOWN BANK BUILDING—THE END OF THE DAY

A vaulted Art Deco affair, touched with a "middle-American" flavor. An endless expanse of TELLERS *and* CUSTOMERS *finishing up for the day. The sound of business being transacted is deafening.*

HOWARD *is moving between the brass gates, sneaking in just as the* GUARD *is about to close up.* HOWARD *starts zigzagging back and forth. He is looking for something. Occasionally,* PEOPLE *look up but then immediately go back to their jobs. And then he finds her. He stands there a moment until* CHRISTINE *finally notices him. She looks radiant, with her eyes locked on a computer screen and her headphones in place. Her hair is cut in a new style.* HOWARD *steps forward, unable to speak at first. He brings himself to touch her on the shoulder.*

> HOWARD
>
> Listen . . .

CHRISTINE *looks at him momentarily, a flicker of emotion crossing her face. She considers him for the briefest of seconds, then nothing. Her head drops back down to the task at hand.* HOWARD *again tries to gain her attention, his voice slowly escalating.*

> HOWARD
>
> Listen . . . listen . . . listen. . . .

88

HOWARD *is hysterical now, his voice soaring to the heavens. The entire room slowly stops in intervals, heads turning or popping into view from around corners, all eyes turned toward the young man in the expensive overcoat as he bellows over and over. The guard starts to walk toward him but on he SCREAMS.*

HOWARD

. . . Listen! Listen!! Listen!!! Listen!!!! Listen!!!!!

HOWARD*'s voice and the sound of* CHRISTINE *typing are the only noises left, echoing up to the ceiling.* HOWARD *continues to scream.* CHRISTINE *never looks up from her work. The sound suddenly drops out and all that is left is* HOWARD*'s face in closeup, twisted and flaming red as he screams impotently at her, over and over and over.*

TRIBAL MUSIC ROARS IN. SLOW FADE OUT TO
SILENCE. DARKNESS.

Thanks to:

Len Jenkin
Charles Metten
Tim Slover
Robert Nelson

Special Thanks to:

The Sundance Film Festival
South by Southwest Film Festival
New Directors/New Films
Festival International du Film de Cannes
Alliance Independent Films
Electric Pictures
Sony Pictures Classics